D1245367

FAITH IN CITIES

HOW BETTER PLACES
MAKE BETTER NEIGHBORS

CHRIS LAZARO

In memory of my dad, whose love for his neighbor will not be forgotten. And to my son, Caleb, may you always love God and others well.

CONTENTS

FOREWORD

—**ALAN BRIGGS**, author, founder and lead creator at
Stay Forth Designs

"Why is everyone's 'dream home' outside the city?"

I was frustrated to hear another family was moving out of our city. That was the good life for them. And so many others. I've watched the pattern repeat itself: get a promotion at work, save some money, move out of the city into your "dream home." I was frustrated because I had wrestled with the idea myself and come to a different conclusion.

A decade ago, around a dozen of us made a bold decision: to stay. We saw the seeds of greatness being sown in our city. With dreams abounding and limitless possibilities we voluntarily decided to limit ourselves to working for the good of Colorado Springs instead of heading to a bigger metro area.

Our jobs and family makeup have changed, but our posture has not. Our braided stories unfolded in our city. We are civic leaders, business owners, pastors, nonprofit leaders and investors. But the interesting side result is that we've all chosen to know our neighbors. Our neighborhoods have cultivated us, and we've cultivated them.

I've seen stories like ours across the country from Orange County to Pittsburgh to Phoenix to Evansville. It would be a mistake to think this was somehow our idea. The people of Jesus have always lived a thriving, patient faith in cities. From Rome to Ephesus to small cities dotting the Ancient Asia Minor Coast, God's people have found a way to both participate in the life of cities and live a countercultural faith.

City life is in the bloodstream of the Church, but we forgot about this for a season. The Church got entangled in the American Dream and forgot about the needs of cities along the way. Congregations were displaced from their neighborhoods with longer commutes to worship with God's people. The church growth movement didn't celebrate churches thriving amidst the challenges of cities that would never grow to be anything resembling "mega."

But something is changing. Jesus followers are becoming active participants in cities and neighborhoods again. Many are living intentionally among the realities in our cities, not apart from them. Many of them are both living their faith in the realities of cities, but are also gaining faith in cities themselves.

This is a day for gritty, honest conversations about cities. This book is one of those conversations. These pages will bring you a wider vantage about both cities and your faith. Chris Lazaro comes from a unique convergence. His background, education, and love for cities immediately had me listening. He explores topics like justice, economics and design that often don't enter our simplistic ideas of cities.

The precious resource we're all fighting for is time. If you're picking up this book be assured you're investing your time well. You will be challenged, reminded and nudged through this book to keep the faith—in Jesus and your role in cities. In a world shouting, "Go forth!" Lazaro is whispering "stay forth." If you are ready to reconsider your role in the place you reside, this book is for you.

INTRODUCTION

As a child I can recall dreaming up a place I called Youngsterville. It was a terrible name for what seemed to be an incredible concept at the time. In Youngsterville, children lived independently as self-governing, self-sufficient beings. We would ride around our master-planned community in go-karts to get food, have fun with friends, and trick out our very own apartments. You had to be of a certain age to live in Youngsterville, of course. As the name implies, parents weren't allowed, except to visit, but neither were small children. This place was strictly for mature young adults.

I have fond memories of building neighborhoods out of LEGO bricks and Lincoln Logs, lying prone on the carpet, breathing life into Little People, assigning imaginary characters to Hot Wheels cars, and orchestrating their lives like some sort of three-dimensional Sim City game. My brother and I would spend good chunks of our school vacations building and rebuilding these strange soap opera-like communities, turning plastic toys into generations of characters that were not unlike those on *Melrose Place* or *Beverly Hills 90210*.

The more I think of it, the more I realize my passion for places could easily be mistaken for obsession. When I wasn't racing imaginary people through their carpeted communities in a yellow Miata or aqua Jeep Wrangler, I was meticulously designing my independent adult life. I drew out hundreds of floor plans for the home I would eventually build, thinking through where each bedroom would go and where the stairs should lead. I pored over each year's new IKEA catalog, outlining room-by-room which objects I would own and where they would go.

It was that same passion that led me to architecture school as a college freshman. I arrived to the picturesque waterfront campus of Roger Williams University in Bristol, Rhode Island, with more junk and idealism than I could possibly fit into my seven-foot by twelve-foot dorm room. But it didn't take long for me to realize that architecture itself was not my calling. As it turns out, agonizing over the details of some abstract building that will never be built did not light my fire. With that, I reversed course, returning to my home state of Maryland to complete my degree in psychology, an odd choice considering I never actually wanted to work in that field.

I first found my spark at the University of Maryland in a class called Challenge of the Cities, an introductory course in urban planning. I had never heard of urban planning prior to that time, nor had I heard of the woman I would soon learn is a planning legend: Jane Jacobs.

Like many would-be planners, reading her quintessential book, *The Death and Life of Great American Cities,* was a bit of a spiritual experience. I found it difficult to get through the book, not because it was dense but because, page after page, it transported me to the vitality of the city. I would get lost in my imagination each time I picked up the taupe-colored hardback, realizing every so often that I'd stared at the same page for several minutes.

Yet, rather than heading immediately into my advisor's

office to switch my major to Urban Planning, I continued on my path to a psychology degree, later becoming a part-time student to begin a career in kitchen and bath design. As it turns out, I occasionally miss life's clues.

———

I am writing this book because I believe there is a deep connection between my passion for cities and my faith. When we are commanded by God to love our neighbors, I understand this command not just in the abstract—as a general call to be nice to people—but as one that includes loving my literal neighbors.

As a kid, I was unabashed when it came to talking to strangers. I remember striking up conversations with people on the front porch of my apartment building, as they smoked a cigarette or waited for a ride, leaning casually against the red brick wall. It wasn't uncommon for me to make small talk with the nurses at my pediatrician's office or the cashiers at the grocery store. I had become so skilled at adult conversation, in fact, that I would often be mistaken for an adult woman on the phone when telemarketers called, not a scrawny ten-year-old boy.

Connecting with our neighbors was something my parents modeled well for me. First, when we lived in our apartment and, later, when we bought our first house, getting to know our neighbors was a given. It was not uncommon for my mom and dad to spend a half-hour catching up with the family across the street, even before setting foot in their own home after a long day of work. After several summers in our small post-war Cape Cod house, we even brought the patio furniture out to the front yard so that neighbors could join us for the occasional burger and hot dog under the large oak trees.

These connections eventually led to yearly Fourth of July block parties, where extended family, friends, coworkers, and neighbors would join together in our front yard for food, conversation, and laughter. And as it got dark, we would pile into each other's cars to end the evening with one of the area's great fireworks displays.

I now realize that in the 1980s and 90s, what I experienced as a child was unique. I grew up with a Filipino father and a white mother in a predominantly black neighborhood. While cities were expanding into the suburbs by building houses with large garages, my upbringing was decidedly more urban. My family lived a stone's throw from our nation's capital, first in a 1950s-era apartment building and, later, in that small Cape Cod with tan asbestos siding and a built-in flower bed made from brick. There were no cul-de-sacs, no garages, no big-box stores. A short walk led me to places where I could buy snacks, get a haircut, and even catch a second-run movie. Public transportation wasn't just an abstract concept, either. I learned to use it as an adolescent to get to the mall during summer vacations and, eventually, to my first job.

My move to college in Rhode Island was something of a culture shock. There wasn't much to do in Bristol, on or off-campus, and the local bus to Providence ran just once an hour. Freshmen at Roger Williams University weren't allowed to have their own cars, increasing my sense of isolation. On top of that, encountering minorities on campus was the exception rather than the rule. I never made a single black friend that year, and barely knew a soul who wasn't from New England.

———

I like to think that Challenge of the Cities class gave words to explain who I already was, growing up in a multicultural setting and having the privilege of spending time in a variety of places, both across America and across the globe, observing what makes each place great in its own way. In the past decade I have found myself in places like Austin and Amsterdam, Barcelona and Brisbane, Florence and Frankfurt, Oslo and Osaka. In each place I saw not just a collection of buildings, streets, and people, but the physical expression of what it means to be in community. Cities and small towns alike rely on a certain level of togetherness, of cooperation, in order to function effectively.

But beyond just understanding the connections that are inherent in cities, I also sought out what God sees in these places. As a Christian I wanted to know: What is it about cities that reflects His character? How might cities be an answer to His calling on our lives?

This book is a journey that explores the intersection of faith and cities in a way I hope will answer the above questions. I first attempt to define community in concrete terms, not just as a loose collection of people who share similar interests or zip codes, but as lives more deeply connected. I look at how cities have both solved and created problems for humanity, serving both as case studies for how to function, as well as warning beacons for what not to do. Then, I explore the role of the Christian faith in contemporary America, revealing how seemingly unrelated aspects of life and faith do, in fact, impact where and how we live.

When I decided to call this book *Faith in Cities*, I knew that the phrase would have at least two interpretations. First, *Faith in Cities* is about what it means to be a person of faith living in cities. But second, *Faith in Cities* is also about believing in the power of cities themselves, that the collective nature of places has the potential to transform lives for the better.

My hope is that you, as a reader, will end this book with a greater understanding of not just why cities are important, but how our decisions about where we live, where we work, and even what we believe about others, have a ripple effect on our communities.

If you are a part of a local church, my other hope is that this book will help you better understand the intersection of the spiritual and the physical realms, and that you walk away convinced that the Bible has important things to say, not just about how we live and worship, but also where.

CHAPTER 1
CIRCLES & SQUARES

As he stepped out from the church office, he heard a woman's voice floating up from downstairs.

"Does anyone need this box?" she asked, holding an empty carton that had housed a small speaker.

My friend didn't need the box she asked about, but he felt himself wondering if he might regret not taking it. And, although he did decline, it got him thinking.

"Why did I find myself coveting that cardboard box?" he asked himself out loud as he recalled that story to me. "I didn't have any real use for it, but for some reason I felt for a second that I had to have the box."

It sounds strange, but what was otherwise a forgettable exchange between him and that woman turned out to be a foundational moment for him. You see, my friend is from Zimbabwe, a landlocked nation that borders South Africa and, for him, the concept of a box was a bit out of the ordinary.

"In America, everything is about the box," he started. "All the things we buy come in boxes, those boxes are shipped in other boxes, and those boxes are transported in boxes with wheels, arriving to stores that are basically boxes. We sleep in rooms that are shaped like boxes, go to work by driving our own metal boxes, just to arrive at another box where we work for eight hours.

"Zimbabwe is about the circle. The room where I slept was a circle, which was next to other circular buildings arranged in a circle, which were all situated around a larger round building. And when we gathered, it too was in a circle."

Many of our human ancestors—not just in Zimbabwe— built their homes in circular shapes, resembling the shapes we find in nature. As it turns out, round buildings tend to be more energy efficient, more resistant to strong wind gusts from storms, and even use less materials to build.

When I asked my friend what the biggest difference is between communities in America and those in Zimbabwe, I didn't expect such a profound response. In fact, that conversation was a bit of an aha moment for me. For years I had read about the definition of community, as well as the difference between individualistic cultures, like in America, and collectivist ones, like in Zimbabwe. But my picture was incomplete. I had assumed that Americans' rugged individuality was something built into our DNA, and that being Asian or African or South American meant having genes bent toward collectivism. Being the independent Americans we are, it's no wonder we love our homes detached from one another, fences between each one, and cars that are more rolling living rooms than transportation devices. What I have been learning, though, is that how we relate to one another isn't so much about our genetics as it is about our environment.

After lunch with my friend that day, I started to think about my own family. My mother was born in Maryland and spent her childhood in Michigan and upstate New York. My late father, a Filipino, was raised in Manila and immigrated to the U.S. at age

23. I can recall the clash of cultures between them bubbling over on a few occasions, my father not giving a second thought to helping out a sibling overseas by sending a little cash or offering a bed to a visiting parent, while my mother wondered why they had not discussed these things first. To my mother, and to many other Americans, the goal of adulthood is independence from parents and siblings. But to my dad, sharing wealth with relatives is just something you do. There is no deeming a sibling worthy of help, evaluating his ability to "pick himself up by the bootstraps." There is no calling a Howard Johnson when Grandma visits or relying on a taxi to pick her up at the airport.

Things got crowded, too. One summer, my grandparents, aunt, and cousin all traveled from the Philippines to stay with my family, the eight of us in a modest three-bedroom, one-bath house. While it was no big deal for my father, my mom started to lose her cool with all the closeness. The only place she could find solitude, even for a moment, was her bedroom: a nine-foot-by-ten-foot room that barely fit a queen size bed and wardrobe. What was supposed to be a long-term living arrangement lasted just two months.

—

In the traditional sense, community is defined as a collection of people living with or near each other: roommates sharing a house, homeowners in a single subdivision, tenants in a single apartment building, residents living in the same small town. The scale is such that you could reasonably encounter these people in your daily life. Today, however, defining community can seem much more abstract. After all, we sometimes think of Facebook as a community. Crossfit can be labeled as a community. People of a singular ethnic group are seen as a community. Members of each of these communities can be anywhere in the world, oblivious to the very existence of one another. By default, building strong communities with those present in your daily life is much more possible than with those who share a platform, hobby, or nation of origin.

When we look to the Bible for the definition of community, it turns out that scale can also vary. Throughout the Old Testament, the entire nation of Israel was called a community. By the time we reach Acts 2 in the New Testament, we see the earliest Jesus-followers forming their own fast-growing community:

> "All the believers devoted themselves to the apostles' teaching, and to fellowship, and to sharing in meals...and to prayer. A deep sense of awe came over them all, and the apostles performed many miraculous signs and wonders. And all the believers met together in one place and shared everything they had. They sold their property and possessions and shared the money with those in need. They worshiped together at the Temple each day, met in homes for the Lord's Supper, and shared their meals with great joy and generosity—all while praising God and enjoying the goodwill of all the people. And each day the Lord added to their fellowship those who were being saved" (Acts 2:42-47).

These believers in the book of Acts weren't building strong ties through social media or a workout program. Their strength was based on a common identity, as well as on proximity. They met, literally, in each others' homes, attended the same congregations, shopped in the same places, and walked by each other on the same roads. I would bet that each of them knew the address of every other person in their community and could knock on any of their doors for a cup of flour if need be.

For many Americans, though, this Acts 2 idea of community can sound downright scary. Just think how awkward it would be if your next-door neighbor knocked on your front door in hopes that you could spend dinner together—at *your* dinner table.

Nancy was exactly this type of neighbor. She was a tall, thin, older woman, who lived alone in the house across the street from ours in East Riverdale after being widowed at a young age. She had no family in the area and spent much of her time in house clothes, usually a baggy pair of paint-splattered sweatpants and a T-shirt or sweatshirt with a cheeky saying printed on it. You could find her perched at a small kitchen table with her cigarette in a plastic ashtray, fronted by a boxy radio and 13-inch television. She listened to Rush Limbaugh faithfully each afternoon, and repainted her kitchen cabinets every two years to cover the yellowing caused by her smoking habit. Her biggest fear was thunderstorms.

For decades Nancy would take a bus or a cab to the nearest IHOP whenever there was a threat of thunderstorms, and she would sit there, chatting up the waitstaff for hours until any possible storms had passed. If you know anything about summers in the mid-Atlantic, you know we often had thunderstorms, but she needed to be around other people to keep her calm. As Nancy and my family got to know each other better throughout the 1990s, we offered our home as a refuge so that she wouldn't have to travel the mile-and-a-half every time the weatherman called for foul weather. There were many seemingly inconvenient times when she would knock on our front door in that distinctive "shave and a haircut" rhythm to flee the pending storms. She would sometimes eat the food my father cooked, and other times talk over our favorite TV shows. On occasion, we would even set up the couch for her to sleep on, so that we could all go to bed.

As awkward as she sometimes could be, blurting out a cuss word whenever a loud clap of thunder scared her, my family knew that Nancy loved and trusted us. She needed us, really.

You might have a Nancy living near you, that slightly eccentric neighbor who brags about her "genuine Naugahyde recliner," or yells when you park on the street in front of her house (which is public property, by the way). But the sad alternative is knowing none of your neighbors at all. In his book *The Art of Neighboring*, Jay Pathak challenges us to know our literal neighbors—next door, across the street, and even behind us. What are their names? What are a few facts about them that you couldn't know just by observing them from afar? Even for me, this is a challenge. While I grew up knowing my neighbors the way Pathak writes about, being that type of neighbor as an adult has been more difficult.

From the time I left home for college, I've lived at 14 different addresses in nine different cities. Unsurprisingly, then, it isn't easy to build strong connections with those in the house or apartment next door when the likelihood is small that you'll still be living next to them a year from now. I hear many young people make this excuse for not getting close to others. Why try to forge deep relationships with new people when they'll be nothing more than Facebook friends in a few months?

I get it. It hurts to break ties with people you've grown to love. And once you've moved enough times, the pain of leaving good friends behind becomes numbing. Our tendency, then, is to keep our friendships shallow so that we don't have to experience the pain of goodbyes. To avoid the people that are easiest to avoid.

To stay in our boxes, seeing people only through windshields and computer screens. However, I say even deep friendships at risk of loss are better than friendships not forged at all.

For me, one of those friendships is with someone who, more than 15 years later, I still consider one of my best friends. I met Jon while I was living in a temporary arrangement, sharing a townhouse near the University of Maryland with another friend. Jon showed up from Michigan for an internship with NASA Goddard Space Flight Center and by many accounts we should not have become good friends: he would be heading back to Michigan and I would move out of the townhouse in a short couple months. It would certainly have been easier to have kept Jon at a distance.

Jon later graduated and got a job with NASA, relocating to Maryland permanently. We even had the fortune of being housemates again. We came to rely on each other's friendship, through some of the most difficult family circumstances either of us would face, as well as through some of life's greatest moments. When his parents struggled in their marriage, I was there. When I nearly lost my father to a suicide attempt, he was there. When he married the love of his life, I was there. And when I married mine, he was my Best Man.

Meeting my wife also came out of risk. When I moved to Waco, Texas in 2008, sight unseen, my plan was to stay long enough to finish my commitment as an Americorps*VISTA volunteer and move down the road to Austin. For nearly five years I had my eye on Austin, and Waco was meant to be a mere pitstop on the way there. I laughed at friends and family back home when they joked about how I was moving there to find a wife. Just two weeks after my move, I met Tara. Less than three months later, we were dating. Less than a year after that, we were married. Dear family and friends, you were right.

As with many things in life, the reward of relationships is worth the risk. It is worth the nosy neighbors to get to the Fourth of July block parties. It is worth the many goodbyes to get to your forever friends. The risk, though, is not so much in saying hello or chatting about the weather. The risk is in trusting other people and, these days, trust feels expensive.

Researchers and journalists alike have been trying to understand social trust for many years, and particularly why social trust seems to be eroding. The National Opinion Research Center has been asking Americans the same question since 1972: "Generally speaking, would you say that most people can be trusted or that you can't be too careful in dealing with people?" In the survey's first year, about 46 percent of people believed most people could be trusted. Today, that number has fallen to about 31 percent[1]. Yet, the FBI reports that the violent crime rate in America is lower than when NORC's first survey was conducted, and remains at about half of its 1991 peak[2].

As human interaction deteriorates, so does social trust, says scientists like Robert Putnam and David Halpern. Conversely, communities with a strong network of neighborly relationships are more likely to benefit from lower crime, better physical and mental health, and better economic growth.

It turns out that religious affiliation also plays a role in social trust, but its effects are complex. A recent study from Saint Mary's University in Nova Scotia found that people who identify with certain denominations tend to trust their neighbors more than those who don't identify with any religion[3]. Some researchers have found that those who attend church regularly tend to be more trusting than those who attend less frequently[4]. Yet, one cross-cultural analysis shows that the nonreligious are more trusting of other people than the religious[5].

For those who identify as Christians, this eroding social trust poses a significant problem. After all, the greatest commandment in Scripture flies in the face of our skepticism of other people:

> "Teacher, which is the most important commandment in the law of Moses?" Jesus replied, "'You must love the Lord your God with all your heart, all your soul, and all your mind.' This is the first and greatest commandment. A second is equally important: 'Love your neighbor as yourself.' The entire law and all the demands of the prophets are based on these two commandments." (Matthew 22:36-40)

Surprisingly, the second half of Jesus' answer to the Pharisees tells us that loving our neighbors is just as important as loving God. But who is our neighbor? Sure, it includes the Nancys and Jons in our lives, but I believe this command extends far beyond just our literal neighbors. Neighbors aren't just the server at your favorite restaurant and the nurse who gives your child an extra sticker just to see him smile; they are also the driver you yelled at for cutting you off and the homeless man yelling obscenities at the wind outside the local coffee shop. They are your ex-girlfriend, your annoying boss, the friend who never returned your favorite book. They are the ones who write hurtful things on social media, the ones who worship other gods, the ones who worship no god at all. In his book, *On God's Side,* Jim Wallis effectively sums up the neighbor question by writing: "Jesus obliterates all our notions of acceptable boundaries between neighbors…there are no 'nonneighbors' in this world."

On the surface, it seems that most Christians agree with Wallis' statement—that loving our neighbors, literal or otherwise, is good. According to the Pew Research Center, nine out of 10 Christians say that churches and other religious organizations play a key role in helping the poor and needy[6]. And 92 percent say churches help bring people together in a way that strengthens neighborhoods. The *Chronicle of Philanthropy* discovered that Christians also give more to charitable organizations, including both religious and mainstream institutions (It is worth noting, however, that when giving to churches is excluded, the non-religious actually outgive Christians)[7]. Data shows that Christians also volunteer their time more often than the non-religious[8].

For many of us, the realization that all of humanity is our neighbor can overwhelm us to the point that we'll say we love them, all while continuing to avoid most people on any given day. Living in a society full of boxes makes it incredibly easy to do just that. Nationally, more than three-quarters of American workers drive alone to work. The majority of households live in detached single-family homes. And although I'm not making a claim that driving to work and living in single-family homes are inherently bad, I am arguing that the way in which we have built out our country in the last half-century directly impacts how we behave toward one another.

Close to 80 percent of drivers in America admit to driving aggressively during the past year, according to the AAA Foundation for Traffic Safety[9]. Worse, the same survey revealed that about 8 million drivers actively engaged in road rage, which includes hitting another vehicle on purpose or actively confronting another driver. Eric Jacobsen said it best in his book, *Sidewalks in the Kingdom*: "Driving brings out the worst side of being human in us. Other drivers, instead of being neighbors whom we greet, are competitors with us for limited lane space and parking." Sadly, I can relate. I would never say I have the patience of Job, but one merely needs to be a fly in my car to see my true colors.

You might be thinking, "But I'm a private person when it comes to my faith." I understand. The idea of private Christianity makes sense. After all, Matthew 6:6 tells us to pray in private. Even Jesus took time away from people to be alone. Focusing on our private disciplines is a good and necessary thing. But I would argue that we have slowly allowed privacy to overshadow our call to outward-focused faith. Mark Dever, a pastor in Washington, D.C., said in an interview with *Christianity Today* that many churches do not reflect a strong sense of community, leading to the false understanding that "Christianity is very private."[10] In the same interview, Jim Wallis added:

> "...Matthew 25 says the sheep and the goats are separated not based on their theology, or their doctrine, or their church membership, or their position on this or that. It's how they treat those who are hungry, thirsty, naked, sick, and a stranger. 'As you've done to the least of these, you've done to me,' Jesus said...That passage brought me back to Christ; it brought me back to my personal faith because I saw that faith was not just about 'me and Jesus' but about the world."

Some modern churches seem to be promoting private Christianity, perhaps in an effort to attract younger generations that appear less interested in God, or at the very least in traditional worship styles. For some of these churches, success is not defined by whether it has preached a complete gospel or whether its attendees are actively living out their faith. Rather, they see success through a consumer-driven model, where each service is meticulously designed to keep its audience entertained and coming back for more. This is not to condemn the slick production and lighting, or the lobby cafes, but rather to ask whether these elements promote a biblical community or simply a brand.

How did the idea of private faith develop anyway? Norman Wirzba, Professor of Theology and Ecology at Duke University explored this question recently in *The Huffington Post*. He argues that the privatization of faith occurs when we worry more about being seen as judgmental than about the integrity of our beliefs[11]. The stance that your faith is only between you and God "has widespread sympathy," Wirzba said, "because it is easy to appreciate how scary and uncivil our world would become if everyone made it his or her business to cast judgment on the authenticity of the lives of others." He goes on further:

> "Though faith clearly is a *personal* matter...it is a mistake to believe that faith is a *private* matter. Why? Because when faith is reduced to the private domains of life it ceases to have public and broadly interpersonal effect...Jesus put it plainly when he told his followers to love others as he loved them...[He] does not call people to the cozy confines of the home or church. He calls them to go out into the world to share love rather than hate, and to practice humility and mercy rather than arrogance and belligerence... Christian faith is not reducible to the relationship between an individual person and his or her God. It is a relationship that grows, and is shown to be true or false, in the love people show to each other."

Living out the Christian faith in public can be pretty messy, too. Social media is filled with well-meaning Christians blogging out their feelings about the latest unbiblical legislation, imploring their friends to boycott a corporation because of its position on controversial issues, and condemning others for voting this way or that. Even leaders in the faith express perplexing views when we view them through the lens of the Bible and through the life of Jesus. But what I find encouraging is when people of different denominations, different faiths, and even those with no particular faith at all, come together for the common purpose of loving people. A silver lining of social media is that these examples can be found there as well.

When Superstorm Sandy wrecked the northeast in 2012, people turned to social media to seek—and receive—help from relief organizations. Likewise, social media has helped mobilize volunteers to donate blood, clean up debris, and assist families with practical needs in the aftermath of the 2010 Haiti earthquake and the 2013 typhoon in the Philippines. Following Hurricane Harvey, which dumped 51 inches of water on the Houston area in 2017, laymen used social media to organize groups to rescue those trapped by the floodwaters. A couple days after the storm had passed, I saw a parking lot in San Antonio filled with flat-bottomed boats hitched to pickup trucks, with men and women all ready to deploy help.

Perhaps one of the biggest humanitarian crises of our time, though, is what has been happening in the nation of Syria. Since the Syrian civil war began in 2011, more than 5 million people have fled the widespread chaos that has devastated the nation's infrastructure and building stock, and leaving millions of others in desperate need of aid[12]. Though an accurate death toll is nearly impossible to determine, most estimates now say that more than 500,000 have died in the war.

The ways in which we respond to crisis situations hint that we were made for a more "circular" way of life; that is, not just to live our daily lives in the private domain of our homes and our cars, or in a privatized me-and-God type of faith, but rather to experience the spontaneous joy of interacting with other people. Besides, if each and every human being is truly designed in the image and likeness of God, should we not then be clamoring for the chance to get to know them more, just like we are destined to know their Creator?

In the church context, think of the relatively recent phenomenon of small groups. When churchgoers imagine a small group, these groups tend to be seated in a circle. In fact, most discussion groups are deliberately designed so that each participant is seated in a circle. Why? Not only does it make it easier for each person in the circle to see everyone else, it signifies that there is no singular leader. Each person has value, and each person has the ability to contribute to the conversation.

Similarly, round dining tables, as opposed to rectangular ones, offer a more intimate experience for those eating there because it is easier to make eye contact with everyone else. Literally no one is relegated to a corner, cut off from the conversation being held at the other end of the table.

Throughout this book I will explore this "circular" way of living: how we designed ourselves away from it, how we can get ourselves back there, and why it all matters.

CHAPTER 2
THERE GOES THE NEIGHBORHOOD

The idea of attending a public meeting can sound dry, even downright boring. But, if you've ever attended a public meeting about a new development being planned in your community, you probably have a good idea about how contentious these meetings can be. It is not uncommon for residents to yell, curse, or cry—sometimes all three—during the course of one session. Typically residents who show up to these meetings are opposed to new development, citing all sorts of reasons why such places will damage their neighborhood. Often, there are fears that development will bring traffic to a halt, making it impossible to drive through the community or to find parking. There are sometimes concerns about "neighborhood character," opponents worried that new buildings might be *too* different from what is already there, risking the perceived value of their homes.

I have also seen residents oppose new development on the belief that more people make communities less safe. Across North America, you can find newspaper clippings citing resident opposition to new housing, shopping centers, parks, and public transit lines, based on fears that criminal activity will materialize in their neighborhood. One *Houston Chronicle* article highlighted the unfounded belief by some residents that extending bus service to a northern Harris County, Texas suburb would "give criminals an easy way in and out."[1] A resident from an Atlanta suburb was quoted in the *Clayton News Daily*, referring to some transit riders as "unsavory people."[2]

But, what does our resistance to new development communicate? What might it say about how we view others? What unintended consequences might our opposition create?

Much of the time, the reasons cited for opposing development are unwarranted. For instance, an oft-cited reason for opposing apartments is the traffic they will generate. Certainly development will bring more cars than a site that remains undeveloped, but rarely do conveniently-located properties remain vacant forever. While it might seem that apartments exacerbate traffic congestion, apartment dwellers own fewer cars, on average, than those living in single-family houses. According to the Joint Center for Housing Studies at Harvard University, single-family households actually generate more vehicle trips than apartments do[3].

The belief that apartments depress nearby home values—and, in particular, apartments that serve lower-income populations—has also been shown to be a myth. The same Harvard University study cited multiple researchers who came to the same conclusion: not only do multifamily developments have no negative impact on property values for nearby single-family homes, in some places they are associated with higher-than-average increases in home values over time. In 2016, the popular real estate website Trulia released the results of a study that considered the effects of low-income family housing on property values in the 20 least affordable housing markets in the country[4]. What did they find? "There is no statistically significant difference in price per square foot when comparing properties near a low-income housing project and those farther away," according to Trulia. Put more plainly, living near lower-income families doesn't negatively impact property values.

All the controversies I bring up here belie an important observation: the majority of neighborhood opposition to development tends to come from homeowners, not renters. Before we dismiss renters and other apartment dwellers as inherently indifferent to development, I should point out the coincidental rise in homeowner advocacy with the rise in American homeownership. Through 1940, and at least as far back as 1890, fewer than half of Americans owned their homes[5]. It wasn't until the mid-1940s that the majority of Americans could call themselves homeowners, even though many places like Newark, New Jersey, Miami, Florida, and Cincinnati, Ohio remain majority-renter cities. As of 2018, the U.S. homeownership rate sits closer to 65 percent, after peaking at just over 69 percent during the housing bubble of the mid-2000s.

The American pursuit of owning a home was no accident—it was engineered. In 1934, the Federal Housing Administration was created as part of President Roosevelt's National Housing Act in order to make home mortgages more affordable. At least in the aftermath of the stock market crash of 1929, this move made sense. By some estimates, as many as half of home mortgages were in default[6]. This was especially problematic since, unlike today, most private lenders required down payments of about half a home's purchase price, meaning that huge personal wealth was at risk of being lost.

Rise of the American Dream

In his 1931 book *Epic of America*, James Truslow Adams first defined the American Dream as "that dream of a land in which life should be better and richer and fuller for every man, with opportunity for each according to his ability or achievement... regardless of the fortuitous circumstances of birth or position."

In the decades following the Great Depression, Adams' phrasing would come to embody so much more about the American experience. It became evident that success wasn't measured merely by whether people had reached their potential, but by whether they had the ability to purchase the things they were increasingly being told they needed.

Of course, homeownership became the cornerstone of the American Dream during that era, in which every family strove to have its own home with a fence, a yard, and a driveway. Home builders, manufacturers, and the federal government alike began normalizing the now-iconic suburban lifestyle through its artist-drawn advertisements, promising the good life to those returning from combat. Lee Rubber & Tire Corporation called homeownership "fundamental for normal and continued prosperity."[7] Levitt and Sons called its new development in Pennsylvania, "the most perfectly planned community in America," ensuring its homebuyers would find privacy and more leisure time there[8]. A 1940s advertisement by home appliance maker Kelvinator was a bit more flowery with its promise of happiness:

> "There'll come a day when our dreams come true...And the hopes and plans for a house of our own take shape on our land on the edge of town where the frozen brook makes a silver streak between the willows bowed with snow...The kettle will be humming a tune on the range...that wonderful, magical electric range you can leave to cook dinner all by itself."[9]

Throughout the second half of the 20th Century, it seemed that society increasingly revolved around the love of the home. By the 1980s, early shelter magazines like *Architectural Digest*, *Better Homes and Gardens*, and *House Beautiful* were joined by many other popular titles, like *Elle Decor*, *Metropolitan Home*, and *Southern Living*. Home improvement became a mainstay on television screens, with shows like the **PBS** programs *This Old House* and *Hometime*, premiering in 1979 and 1986 respectively. Following the surprise success that was the early-2000s reality-based make-over show, *Trading Spaces*, an entire cable network exploded in popularity, spawning **HGTV** cultural favorites like *House Hunters* and *Fixer Upper*. In the 20-plus years since HGTV's launch, the network would come to be piped into more than 96 million homes worldwide.

Yet, no one sells the promise of homeownership quite like the real estate industry itself. According to the Association of Real Estate License Law Officials, there are about two million licensed real estate agents in the U.S.[10] Most of them have learned the plethora of codewords to ensure that even the country's worst homes appeal to someone. For example, if you find the word "cozy" in a real estate listing, it might mean that the home is small. While contracting your own custom kitchen may sound like a dream, seeing the word "custom" in a listing probably means at least some element of the home is very taste-specific and not likely to appeal to a broad audience. Not long ago, I heard an advertisement for a new subdivision in Austin, Texas that was marketed as being "close to downtown." The subdivision is well over 10 miles from the Texas capitol building, and comes with a daily morning commute that Google estimates could take as long as 45 minutes.

Speaking of new homes, builders themselves have led the way to the current incarnation of American communities. If the U.S. government engineered the American Dream of home-ownership, it was the National Association of Home Builders' members that brought that engineering to life. Home builders have constructed an average 1.4 million homes each year since 1959[11]. The biggest increase in home building occurred in the 1970s, reflecting the time period when Baby Boomers were reaching adulthood. Nearly 20 million homes were constructed between 1970 and 1980.

Yet, the number of homes built since World War II isn't nearly as remarkable as what was built. In 1940, nearly 25 percent of homes were in buildings that architect Daniel Parolek now calls Missing Middle Housing: townhomes, duplexes, triplexes, and fourplexes[12]. Today, these account for just 14 percent of all housing units. The most prevalent housing type, the detached single-family home, also evolved. In 1950, the average home size was a modest 1,000 square feet. Now, the typical single-family home is two-and-a-half times larger, despite the fact that the average household has shrunk[13].

Another remarkable change in homebuilding was the addition of the garage. While early car storage was detached from the home, by the early 1950s, the attached garage had become commonplace, replacing the front entry as the most important door in the house. Along with technology that allowed home-owners to open their garage door with the push of a button, by the 1970s more than half of new homes in America featured a two-car garage. Today, the trend has reached its apex. A 2016 *Bloomberg* article revealed that we're now building more three-car garages than one-bedroom apartments. That article's tagline is perhaps most telling: "you'll never be homeless in America if you're a car."[14]

Despite our many advancements in technology, the promises of homeownership have yet to reach every corner of society. While as many as two-thirds of renters choose to rent for lifestyle purposes, others see that the choice of homeownership just isn't an option for them.

Minorities and the American Dream

Few African-American families owned their homes prior to the 20th Century. Professors William Collins and Robert Margo wrote that, by the turn of the century, roughly one in five black males owned a home, compared to nearly half of white males[15]. By 1960, 66 percent of white households owned their homes, while the same was true for just 39 percent of black families.

Legal restrictions and real estate practices prevented minorities from buying homes in many neighborhoods, contributing to the homeownership gap between whites and minorities. The Federal Housing Administration actually rated neighborhoods based on their supposed financial risk, grading neighborhoods from 'A' to 'D,' with 'A' areas considered the most financially secure and 'D' areas considered the most risky for investment. These areas were marked on maps, with 'A' areas colored in green and 'D' areas colored in red. As a result, mortgages were hard to come by in the red areas, which led to the term "redlining."

It was no coincidence that the 'A' areas were overwhelmingly white and the 'D' areas were mostly Black or Latino. According to one report, as many as 8 in 10 properties in Chicago and Los Angeles in the 1940s included a racial covenant that prohibited black families from buying or residing in them[16]. The words, "no negroes," were printed on many advertisements for new neighborhoods across the nation. Government documents cited "negro infiltration" as a threat to communities.

While racially-restrictive covenants were outlawed in 1948 and redlining was made illegal with the Civil Rights Act, minority homeownership remains low in America*[17]. And for those minority families who do seek to own a home, the barriers they face remain high. The Fair Housing Center of Greater Boston reports that black and Hispanic families are "shown fewer homes and told about fewer listings, asked more questions about their qualifications, steered to other communities,...quoted higher loan rates and offered fewer discounts on closing costs."[18] Even relatively wealthy black families were more likely to be given subprime mortgage loans at the height of the mid-2000s housing bubble than white families earning far less[19].

Among minority homeowners, the equity they hold in their properties is significantly lower than the equity held by whites. Not only that, Emily Badger reported in the *Washington Post* that predominantly black neighborhoods not only lost more of their home values in the late 2000s housing bust, they also did not regain their homes' values in the subsequent recovery[20]. Badger made an insightful observation, as to why this phenomenon may be occurring: "Predominantly black neighborhoods additionally struggle from a smaller pool of demand, because non-black home buyers are less likely to look for housing there."

The racial segregation between neighborhoods is something I experienced first-hand growing up in Prince George's County, Maryland. U.S. Census data shows that in 1970, the county was 14 percent black. Today, P.G. County is just 14 percent white. Yet, when you drill down further into the county's neighborhoods,

---

*Just 43 percent of African-American families call themselves homeowners, compared to nearly 73 percent of white families. About 46 percent of Hispanic households own their homes.

the evidence of racial segregation becomes more stark. In Mitchellville, a suburban enclave between Washington, D.C. and Annapolis, more than 84 percent of its residents are black. Other small communities in the central part of the county, like Largo, District Heights, and Suitland, are more than 90 percent black. In the county's northern suburbs, like Bowie or Beltsville, less than half of their population is black. College Park, home to the University of Maryland, is just 18 percent black.

Meanwhile, just as Prince George's County's black population was growing substantially, nearby Washington, D.C. was losing its black residents. More than a half-million African-Americans lived in the nation's capital in 1970, whereas today the black population is just over 300,000. As it turns out, the racial segregation within D.C. is just as pronounced as it is in the suburbs. In Ward 8, the City's southernmost area, more than 90 percent of its residents are black. In Northwest D.C., Ward 3 is almost 80 percent white.

Suburbanization & White Flight

During this period, Washington, D.C. wasn't just suffering the loss of its African American population—it was losing residents of all races and ethnicities to surrounding counties. In fact, many of America's once-top cities have lost its citizens to other communities in the last 60 years. Chicago, America's largest city in 1950, lost more than a quarter of its population between 1950 and 2010, now ranking third in population behind New York City and Los Angeles. Cleveland and Pittsburgh are each at less than half their 1950 populations. Detroit earns the dishonor of having lost the highest actual number of residents—more than 1.1 million—since 1950. Mike Duggan, Detroit's current mayor, hopes to turn the Motor City back from its mass exodus.

"How can all these cities be losing people?" you might ask. After all, the U.S. population has grown substantially over the last 50 years. Where did those people go? The answer is two-fold. The first can be explained by what urban planners and historians call *white flight*, or the phenomenon of white middle-class families leaving cities for new suburbs. For example, Washington, D.C. experienced a rapid expansion into surrounding counties that fueled the region's growth. Nearby Montgomery County, Maryland, quadrupled its population between 1950 and 2000. In metro Detroit, Macomb and Oakland counties grew by more than 1.4 million people combined.

The second phenomenon that occurred, along with white flight, was the boom of Sun Belt cities. With the availability of home air conditioning, wide freeways, and cheap land in the mid-20th Century, cities across the South and West welcomed new residents in record numbers. Austin, Texas, grew from just 88,000 residents in 1940 to roughly 1 million people today. Las Vegas could barely be called a city in 1940, with just 8,400 residents living there. Today, it is the most populous city in Nevada, with more than 600,000 residents. America's second largest city, Los Angeles has added more than 2.5 million people to its population since 1940.

While Sun Belt cities themselves witnessed massive growth since the mid-1900s, the prevalence of open land allowed them to sprawl out far beyond the boundaries of early U.S. cities. In San Antonio, where I live, recent land annexations make it nearly four times the size of Philadelphia and more than 10 times the size of Boston.

Unfortunately, with the unprecedented growth of southern cities came a phenomenon not experienced at the same scale in pre-war cities. While racial segregation remains a concern in communities across the country, income segregation—the separation of neighborhoods by household income—seems to have grown dramatically across Sun Belt cities. According to the Pew Research Center, the three largest metropolitan areas in Texas also happen to be the most segregated regions in America by household income, with San Antonio taking the top spot**[21]. Using slightly different metrics in its 2016 report, the Economic Innovation Group also ranked San Antonio at the top of its list of cities facing the most inequality[22].

The increase in economic segregation over time is also something that is a uniquely Sun Belt problem. Aside from the three top Texas metros, the biggest increases in income segregation can be found in places like Denver, Miami, and Phoenix. A similar study published by Stanford University's Center for Education Policy Analysis revealed that eight of the 10 cities with the largest increases in income segregation are in the South[23].

Sprawled Out

So, what is leading to the stratification of income groups in southern cities like San Antonio? Because we can't tell our real estate agents to search for homes by how much its owners earn, we rely on other cues to get a sense for the economic makeup of

---

**The Pew Research Center developed the Residential Income Segregation Index (RISI) in 2012, which measures the share of predominantly lower-income households living near each other as well as primarily upper-income households living near each other. The higher a region scores on the index, the more similar its neighbors are to each other, economically speaking. The lower the score, the more economically diverse a city's neighborhoods are.. The Dallas-Fort Worth Metroplex scored a 60 out of a possible 200 points, making it the third-most income segregated region in America (the national average was a 46 on the RISI). The Houston metro area ranked second with a score of 61. The top spot on the list was bestowed not-so-lovingly on San Antonio, with a RISI score of 63.

a neighborhood. Zoning and development regulations are the primary tools that make this possible.

Although the advent of land use regulation was for the purpose of keeping sources of land pollution like factories away from places where people lived, the typical zoning document soon morphed into a behemoth set of rules, carefully regulating everything from the size of buildings to the inner workings of a typical street lamp. My own city's zoning document, known as the Unified Development Code, is more than 1,300 pages long and includes some seemingly arbitrary requirements. For example, when building a miniature golf course the minimum number of parking spaces one must provide is one per hole. If your property is in the "Arts and Entertainment District" and you want to open a bed and breakfast, be careful: if your property is on a corner lot, you can offer up to five guest rooms; if not, you can only offer three. And, if you want to start a business from home, forget about launching it from your garage. According to the document, the "use of accessory buildings, garages, or carports for a home occupation is prohibited."[24]

Since the first comprehensive zoning ordinance was adopted a century ago, zoning has ceased to function only as a tool that keeps dirty industries away from our homes and natural resources, but now works to relegate homes and businesses that are only slightly different from each other into distinct pockets of the community. As Eric Jacobsen put it in his book, *Sidewalks in the Kingdom*, modern zoning regulations, "spread us out to the point that we spend more time in our cars than interacting with neighbors. Residential neighborhoods are segregated even at the slightest variation in income, and we have pushed commercial gathering spaces, like coffee shops, away from where we live." And what is the effect of this? Jacobsen continues: "Extreme separation zoning not only segregates types of buildings and people into different areas of the city, it also segregates the time in our day into unrelated bursts of activity punctuated by energy-draining car trips." As a result, even though redlining and racial steering have been outlawed decades ago, seemingly benign zoning regulations continue to deliver the same results.

The suburbanization of America, while delivering for many the benefits of ownership, has managed to deliver a host of negative consequences for its citizens. Though the U.S. population has doubled since 1950, residential and transportation energy use has more than tripled[25]. Commute times to work have increased to the point that the average American commuter spends about 42 hours each year stuck in rush-hour traffic[26]. While just one in ten kids were driven to school in the 1960s, today close to half of children are part of a daily drop-off-pick-up ritual that creates headaches for parents, school officials, and those living near these twice-daily parades. All that time we spend sitting in traffic has widened our waistbands: in 1960, just 14 percent of Americans could be classified as obese[27]. Today, nearly 40 percent of adults are obese[28].

Beyond all that, sprawling development is expensive. For instance, Boston is responsible for maintaining about 800 miles of city streets. Oklahoma City, with a similar population, owns more than 8,000 miles of streets. Washington, D.C. has a staff of 20 arborists to ensure its trees stay healthy throughout its 68 square miles. I was told that, aside from a crew dedicated to maintaining its parks, San Antonio has just four public works staff responsible for all its landscaping citywide, despite having more than twice the population and seven times more land area.

Sprawl isn't just expensive for governments; it's expensive for us. A 2013 report by the Smart Prosperity Institute in

Ontario, Canada found that low-density suburban development costs each household more than twice as much as efficient urban development[29]. Another analysis by consulting firm Fregonese & Associates revealed that low-density sprawl actually costs more to serve with infrastructure and public safety services than it pays the city in taxes, whereas more compact housing pays more in taxes than required for those same services[30].

To be clear, I am not arguing that everyone should live downtown or that it is morally wrong to live in the suburbs. I have lived in a range of neighborhoods over the years and can easily find the good in any of them. What I discovered, however, is that most of us do not actually have as much choice about where we live as we think we do and, thus, live where we do by default.

My wife and I purchased our first home a few years ago, and after months of house hunting and one lengthy contract that fell apart at the last minute, we consider ourselves fortunate to have found a home that matched our tastes and that we could afford to buy in a neighborhood just a couple miles north of downtown San Antonio. The same would not have been possible for us in many costlier cities, including nearby Austin. Even though we like our home and where we live, it was a compromise nonetheless. For buyers like us, who would prefer to live in a townhouse, our options are scarce. Of the half-million homes that exist in San Antonio, less than 3 percent are townhomes; and, for the few townhomes built in recent years, their sales prices far exceeded our budget. Nationally, less than 6 percent of our housing stock are townhouses.

When I first met Daniel Parolek in 2015, I had barely heard the term Missing Middle housing. As I mentioned earlier, it refers to the range of housing types between a conventional apartment property and a detached single-family house, including town-houses, duplexes, and garage apartments. What I learned is that we used to build these in much greater numbers a century ago, but have effectively regulated them out of existence (hence, why they're called *missing*). As we toured the burgeoning Oak Cliff neighborhood of Dallas, I looked past a streetscape of mature Live Oak trees to find dozens of these modestly-scaled buildings with their brick facades concealing two, four, and sometimes up to 12 small apartment units. They sat on grassy residential lots, camouflaged by the many other charming historic homes that housed but one family each. Perhaps some of the residents in the single-family homes see themselves as merely coexisting with the families living in the multi-unit buildings, but I believe the relationship between them is far more symbiotic. The neighborhood's commercial strip, known as the Bishop Arts District, labels itself "Dallas' most independent neighborhood," consisting of "over 60 independent boutiques, restaurants, bars, coffee shops, and art galleries." Normally, such a thriving corridor would depend on having many hip urban midrise and high-rise buildings nearby to keep its businesses open; yet, I cannot even recall a single building taller than three stories in all of Oak Cliff.

Privacy & Hospitality

Over the last hundred years the idea of *home* has come to mean many different things. It was a reward for the servicemen and women who fought for our country's freedoms. It was an escape from the urban ills of the late 19th and early 20th centuries. It was a status symbol of newfound wealth. Today, more and more, it is at once a place to express our individuality, to retreat from the stresses of the outside world, and a monetary investment to be protected from devaluing forces.

It didn't take long for the form of our homes to reflect these values. Now, 6 in 10 Americans live in detached single-family houses. The vast majority of those homes were built in the last 40 years, often characterized by front doors set back far from the street, prominent street-facing garage doors, family living spaces situated at the rear of the home, and backyards wrapped in wooden privacy fences. Even the neighborhoods themselves no longer connect to one another, their winding roads punctuated by the cul-de-sac. Collectively, these elements send the message that the family itself is a private domain not to be bothered.

But, as I discussed in Chapter 1, our lives were not meant to be lived solely in the private realm. In fact, the Bible's call to hospitality is quite clear. In Romans 12, for instance, the Apostle Paul outlined for the Roman church what it means to live transformed by the gospel of Christ. "Don't just pretend to love others," Paul starts in verse 9. "Really love them." This may seem like an obvious command, but when we explore the original Greek language, we see that Paul's command has more weight. According to John W. Carter, author of *The Disciple's Bible Commentary*, the original Greek *agape anhypokritoz* is most directly translated to mean unconditional, sacrificial love that is without hypocrisy. In his commentary, Carter adds:

> "One who expresses *agape* love cannot discriminate among who will receive such love and who will not. *Agape* love describes that love that God has for His creation, one that is not a 'respecter of persons,' or one who does not favor one over another. Christians are to demonstrate unconditional *agape* love because God is demonstrating the same for them. *Agape* love cannot hold a grudge. *Agape* love cannot discriminate against

someone based on their social status, whether it be racial, economic, or for any other distinction."

That unconditional love, then, leads directly to hospitality, as Paul wrote starting in verse 13:

> "Contribute to the needs of God's people, and welcome strangers into your home. Bless people who harass you—bless and don't curse them. Be happy with those who are happy, and cry with those who are crying. Consider everyone as equal, and don't think that you're better than anyone else. Instead, associate with people who have no status." (Romans 12:13-16, CEB)

Our call to hospitality is made even more uncomfortable when Jesus attends a dinner party in Luke 14, turning to address the dinner host himself:

> "When you put on a luncheon or a banquet... don't invite your friends, brothers, relatives, and rich neighbors. For they will invite you back, and that will be your only reward. Instead, invite the poor, the crippled, the lame, and the blind. Then at the resurrection of the righteous, God will reward you for inviting those who could not repay you." (Luke 14:12-14)

Our tendency, then, to build communities in a way that favors private wealth over those with lesser means sits in contrast to our call to unconditional, welcoming love. What might we be trading when we choose the home in the gated community with the privacy fence? When we pull our automobiles into the garage, closing the door to retreat into the rear of our homes, what opportunities might we have missed to love the stranger as though they were family? Who do our homeowners' association rules protect, and who do they exclude? And when we, as Christians, engage in the opposition of new development itself, we must be honest with ourselves: are we against a development because it legitimately risks harming the community, or are we opposed because the presence of strangers threatens a social order we, directly or indirectly, support? A neighborhood may be rightly justified in resisting the construction of a chemical plant or a landfill near where people live. But who suffers most when homes are prevented from being built, especially housing for families in need? What consequences might we be creating if we insist that the school or the grocery store be located far away from our homes?

CHAPTER 3
THE RETURN TO CITIES

While suburbanization has dramatically altered our landscape over the past 80 years, not everyone with the means to flee to the suburbs has chosen to do so. In fact, most central cities in the U.S. are more than a decade into an urban renaissance, or what author Alan Ehrenhalt calls "The Great Inversion."[1] Washington, D.C., has regained more than 100,000 residents over the last 15 years. Seattle has not only seen a resurgence in its downtown, its core has remained the fastest growing area in the city since 1990. In 2000, downtown Denver was home to about 12,000 residents; today, an estimated 27,000 call its downtown neighborhoods home.

The majority of urban core neighborhoods have grown since the turn of the millennium, and that growth isn't just limited to large, cosmopolitan cities. Des Moines, Iowa, a relatively small Midwestern city, has added more than 10,000 new residents to its downtown since 2000, topping a surprising number of best-city lists. Downtown Pittsburgh, Pennsylvania has turned things around, too, growing its Central Business District, locally known as the Golden Triangle, by more than a third in just five years. And, although it began its renaissance a bit later than other cities, Waco, Texas is seeing a resurgence in its downtown as well. According to Chris McGowan, consultant and former Director of Urban Development for the Greater Waco Chamber of Commerce, about 3,000 new residents have moved to Waco's downtown area in the last decade. For context, the City of Waco's population has grown by roughly 10,000 in that same time period.

In 2008, Waco became my home for three years. I moved to the city, knowing no one and bringing only what I could fit in my old, gold Volvo. I had never been to Waco before, and knew practically nothing about it. Despite the unknown, I was privileged to arrive in Waco at a time when people began paying more attention to a downtown that had been ravaged by a F-5 tornado in 1953, killing 114 people and injuring 600 others. More than 50 years had passed since there was any significant private investment in downtown[2].

Driving over the Brazos River into Downtown a decade ago, I looked toward Waco's modest skyline and said to myself aloud, "Wow, this place has so much potential." As it turns out, I wasn't the only one to think that. The following year, Chris McGowan would lead our city in a process that would be called *Imagine Waco*, a plan for greater downtown. I had never participated in an urban planning exercise before, but I was enthralled. During the inaugural workshop, known as a charrette, I cut out small pieces of cardstock along with others at my table, each cardstock shape representing a type of development we would like to see in our urban neighborhoods. After sometimes intense deliberation, our group glued the cardstock onto the maps, using colored markers to highlight other amenities on our wish list, like bike paths and a streetcar line. I hoped, naively, that our vision for Waco's downtown would become reality...and fast.

I can't recall the way my group laid out Waco's downtown

during that charrette, but things have certainly changed in the city since. New apartments began springing up, including the historic conversion of the 1910-built Waco High School into loft-style apartments. Local developers bought and converted several vacant commercial spaces into places that families now call home. In 2014, Baylor University officially relocated its suburban football stadium to the edge of downtown. Adding to Waco's downtown growth, nearby Chip and Joanna Gaines' Magnolia Market became Texas' second-most visited tourist attraction in 2017, nearly beating the Alamo[3].

Gentrification & Concentrated Poverty

The Great Inversion continues to help revitalize formerly-disinvested cities across the country. Even where I am sitting now, I can see construction occurring across the street on a multi-story apartment building along San Antonio's River Walk. Yet, not everyone welcomes this urban renaissance with open arms. As central neighborhoods grow in their popularity because of things like historic building stock, shorter commutes, and proximity to chic restaurants and entertainment venues, rents and home values also tend to increase, making it challenging for some long-time residents to stay in these neighborhoods. Some even find the rapid change to bring about a clash of cultures, where minorities who have lived in the area for decades feel they no longer have access to the goods or amenities that serve their needs.

The most extreme examples of this change, commonly referred to as gentrification, can be identified in large coastal cities like New York and San Francisco, where median rents have exploded in the last 15 years. Neighborhoods like Greenwich Village and West Village in Manhattan now have median rents fast approaching $4,000 a month[4], while even typical one-bed-room apartments in San Francisco have monthly rents in excess of $3,500[5]. In the ultra-desirable Park Slope neighborhood of Brooklyn, homes have more than doubled in value since 2010[6].

In Portland, Oregon, the cost of living has ballooned as well. A historic townhouse in the Pearl District that sold for $435,000 in 2000 sold in October 2016 for $3.1 million[7]. Rents in Portland have risen at twice the rate of wage increases since 2000[8]. The same is true for Austin. And Denver. And Salt Lake City.

Gentrification can be found, to some degree, in cities across the U.S. I witnessed the phenomenon in Detroit in 2016, where thriving neighborhoods lay side-by-side with withering ones. The front of my Airbnb rental faced a bustling Whole Foods Market that opened in 2013, while the rear of the home pointed toward blocks of mostly vacant lots wrapped in chain-link and coated in tall prairie grass. Peter Moskowitz reflects on the state of Detroit in *The Guardian*: "Boomtown and icon of ruinous decline – to say these two Detroits co-exist would be too optimistic. Separated by as little as a city block, the new Detroit and the rest of Detroit feel like two completely different cities – physically close, far apart in everything else: education, income, outlook on their future."[9]

Some writers take their disdain for this type of neighbor-hood change to near-Shakespearean proportions, crafting prose that would make any reader fear it as disease. Anis Shivani wrote his diatribe in 2014, lamenting change in Houston's Montrose community, a century-old neighborhood just west of downtown. According to Shivani,

> "Houston has transmogrified into a city ruled by a
> brutal strain of neoliberalism, and the city's well-
> known tendency to be disrespectful of history has
> been taken to gothic extremes. It took only a few

short years for developers to displace the original population of the central neighborhoods, while converting the core city into an exclusive play-land for the rich."[10]

Vann Newkirk II wrote about the change he witnessed in his Petworth neighborhood in Washington, D.C., pegging grocery stores more as "agents of gentrification and potential weapons of cultural violence against the poor than as saviors for our country's obesity epidemic."[11]

It is important to be sensitive to the impacts of gentrification taking place across the country. Yet, in many instances, the change that cities are experiencing doesn't warrant such brutal language. In fact, stories of bodegas-turned-cafes are more the exception than the rule. According to researcher Joe Cortright, concentrated poverty has proven a bigger problem over the last 40 years than gentrification. His 2014 study revealed that poor neighborhoods tend to stay poor and, in fact, far more neighborhoods have fallen into poverty in that time period than those impacted by gentrification[12].

Though uncommon and often exaggerated, the impacts of gentrification should not be dismissed wholesale. Those who are displaced by increasing rents as a result of new investment need compassionate action, particularly by their Christian neighbors. In 2015 Deidra Riggs wrote: "We are agents of redemption and partners with God in the work of restoration—not just for houses and properties and cities, but for people who live within the cities we seek to help thrive. This is the work of the Kingdom: bringing light and hope where there is darkness, fear, and hopelessness."[13]

My own desire to partner with God in His work of restoration is what led me to my work in housing policy. According to one estimate, my city is in need of more than 150,000 units of quality affordable housing[14]. While our homeless population is but a small fraction of that number, what this represents are those who are what I call "housing insecure." That is, those who are living in substandard conditions or paying too large a share of their income to stay housed. Many are on years-long waiting lists for the few affordable units that ever get built. Families like these are but a roof leak or broken ankle away from living on someone else's couch or on the streets. Some bounce from one bad apartment to the next, exposing children to instability in their education. Certainly many of these families live in neighborhoods struggling with the side effects of concentrated poverty: failing schools, crumbling infrastructure, and so on. Others, however, are seeing investment happen around them and are now vulnerable because their neighborhoods are at risk of gentrifying.

As it turns out, neighborhoods are delicate places. Where there's too little investment, neighborhoods decay. Where investment happens rapidly, there is fear that long-time residents will be displaced. In neighborhoods with any semblance of stability, there is a tendency to oppose change altogether, or what Benjamin Schwarz eloquently calls an attempt "to render fixed and solid that which inexorably melts into air."[15]

Maintain or Grow?

Keeping neighborhoods intact and functioning is a complex task. Our homes are part of an intricate network of streets, sidewalks, pipes, wires, and services, each needing specialized maintenance. Asphalt streets need to be repaved every 15 years or so, but of course trash must be picked up every week. Hopefully your home will never need the services of the local fire department, but it must be located nearby, just in case. Something we don't often realize, though, is that the more dispersed the network of infrastructure and services, the more expensive it is to build and maintain. A home located on a wide plot of land needs more sewer pipe than one on a narrow lot. The more twists and turns a neighborhood has in its street network, the more fuel it takes for a garbage truck to pick up all the trash. Every dead-end street and cul-de-sac makes it even more challenging for emergency vehicles to reach your home, necessitating additional fire and police resources to ensure rapid response times.

As we've experimented with building dispersed communities that sprawl out into the hinterlands, governments are now realizing just how difficult it is to stave off decay and insolvency with the limited property taxes they receive from property owners. Ask any city or state public works department, and they will tell you that the number of potholes needing to be patched and the miles of streets needing to be repaired cannot be matched by the number of tax dollars available to do so.

Yet, when faced with whether to maintain existing roads or expand them to accommodate future growth, most states choose the latter. Smart Growth America reported that between 2009 and 2011, states spent 25 percent more on roadway expansions than on repairing existing roads[16]. This is particularly ironic, considering that nearly every major roadway expansion results in similar, if not worse, levels of traffic congestion in just a few years time. The most extreme example of this induced demand: the Katy Freeway, west of Houston. The Texas Department of Transportation spent $2.8 billion adding capacity to the highway—to 26 lanes in all, making it America's widest freeway. Unfortunately, all that money didn't seem to help. "More lanes simply invited more cars," Eric Jaffe explained in *CityLab*, "and by 2014, morning and evening travel times had increased by 30 and 55 percent, respectively, over 2011."[17] Rather than learn from this, TxDOT now plans to spend more than $7 billion expanding another freeway in Houston and displacing thousands of residents and workers[18].

The Road to Zero

While on a lunch break back in 2011, I was rear-ended by a driver in a black pickup truck. I was stopped at an intersection and waiting to turn left when she hit me from behind, distracted by her cell phone. While neither of us were hurt in the incident, the Volvo my wife affectionately called Zelga didn't quite pull through. My instinct was to immediately replace the car with another, and I began hopping from dealership to dealership, browsing, test-driving, and calculating the costs. In the back of my mind, though, I kept getting the sense that buying a car wasn't the right thing to do. I'm not sure if that voice was God or Dave Ramsey, but ultimately my wife and I chose to carpool for a while, knowing we could always buy later if it didn't work out.

Candidly, that first month was pretty tough. I was used to the freedom of leaving for work when I wanted to, as was my wife. Coordinating with one another to make sure the car was available for off-site meetings and lunch appointments seemed to be a hassle. What if I was ready to go home but she wasn't? After about a month, though, things started to click. We found a schedule that worked well for both of us, we learned the habit of communication to make sure we always had the car when we needed it during the day, and we learned patience when the other needed to work a little late. The savings from losing one car, which AAA estimates at over $9,000 per year, became palpable[19].

When I opted to go car-free a second time after moving to

San Antonio, I came to rely on our public transit system for my daily commute. I found that, not only is our bus system more affordable than driving, riding the bus freed me up to spend time doing other things, like reading. The stress of navigating traffic and maintaining a car had vanished.

I also learned a lot about the difficulties people face when they have no choice but to live without their own vehicle. I used our bus system for two years, learning both its quirks and its failures. If you're fortunate enough to live and work along a single major route, riding the bus is convenient. Several of our bus lines run every 15 minutes, and one popular route runs every 10 minutes, virtually eliminating the need to check a bus schedule. But, many of our bus stops do not connect to sidewalks, forcing riders to walk on dirt paths, along busy highways, and beside freight railroads. Routes don't often connect to where riders need to go, forcing transfers that can add significant delay to people's commutes, especially along routes where buses only come once an hour. Buses are often late during rush hour or when incidents occur along the route and, in rare cases, I have experienced buses failing to show up at all. It's not uncommon for some of our neighbors to spend as many as four hours a day just riding the bus to and from work or medical appointments.

When we build our communities so that a car is required to access the most basic of needs, we don't just make life difficult for those with low incomes or for those with disabilities, we create challenges for drivers and non-drivers alike. The long-held belief that the automobile offers freedom and independence also adds a mathematical problem: all our cars simply don't fit on the roads. The automobile "is an instrument of freedom that has enslaved us," said Jeff Speck in *Walkable City*. What may be a five-minute drive to a pharmacy for you could be a two-hour journey for someone arriving there by bus. Widening a roadway to shorten your commute by one or two minutes may mean that others' homes were demolished to clear the way.

The faster we believe we should drive to get to our destinations, the more lives we allow to perish on our roadways. As our driving speeds increase, our likelihood of dying in a crash rises exponentially[20]. The result: about 40,000 people die in traffic-related crashes in the United States each year and, as recently reported in *The Washington Post*, more Americans have been killed on our roadways since 2000 than perished in both World Wars combined[21]. Globally, about 1.35 million people die in traffic incidents each year[22].

When we make the effort to protect the lives of people on our roads, however, progress is made. Across America and the world, governments, technology companies, and advocates alike are taking action to curb traffic deaths. Vision Zero, a campaign to eliminate fatalities on our roads, started in Sweden back in 1997 with the core belief that "there is no moral justification for any loss of life in traffic."[23] The premise is that human error is inevitable and, thus, our streets should be designed (or redesigned) to withstand our mistakes without endangering ourselves and others. Today, Vision Zero initiatives have passed in many cities, where some are already seeing positive results. Traffic deaths in New York City fell to a record low in 2018, the fifth year in a row that saw a reduction in roadway fatalities, thanks in part to their Vision Zero efforts[24]. This drop occurred despite continued population growth and the rapid increase in people bicycling.

This type of action should inspire Christians because we are called to value people as God values people. When our cities call for a moral end to traffic violence, the Church should be the first to answer in resounding agreement because God created us in his image (Gen. 1:26-27) and because we would also want others to protect us from unnecessary harm (Matt. 7:12). Unfortunately, some pastors have spoken out against the implementation of Vision Zero in their own communities, worried that swapping parking with bike lanes is a threat to their congregations. One pastor from Brooklyn, New York, publicly called his city's Vision Zero program "insensitive to seniors" and "indicative of an unwise, counter-productive, and undemocratic approach."[25] Another group of pastors from Washington, D.C. expressed worry that the addition of protected bike lanes in the neighborhood might drive their churches out of the area[26].

Conclusion

Is there an ideal neighborhood in which Christians should live? Unfortunately, the answer isn't made clear for us in Scripture. As I said, my goal is not to convince you personally to move to the center city, but to recognize how our decisions regarding place impact how we relate with our neighbors, friends, and family, and also how they affect ourselves and our planet. For some, that will, in fact, result in relocation. For others, it means rethinking our daily routines to open ourselves to the possibilities that come from loving others as Christ loves us. Cities in and of themselves are not necessarily the silver bullet, as Timothy Keller highlighted in *Center Church*:

> "The biblical view of cities is neither hostile nor romantic. Because the city is humanity inten-sified— a magnifying glass that brings out the very best and worst of human nature— it has a dual nature. That is why the Bible depicts cities

as places of perversion and violence and also as
places of refuge and peace...It highlights how the
capacities of this positive social form can be real-
ized for God's glory yet also demonstrates how it
can be a vehicle for enhancing human rebellion
against God."

It will take deliberate action on my part and on yours
to make our communities, big and small, "places of refuge
and peace." It will take heeding Jay Pathak's call to know our
neighbors, as I mentioned in Chapter 1. It will take seeing how
neighbors with lesser means are forced to experience our communities, while also advocating for changes that render justice
to them. It will take understanding how our neighbors of color
have been excluded from opportunities to fully participate in
our society—even as laws have changed—and committing to be
inclusive. It will take showing up to those same public meetings
where opposition is commonplace, speaking instead in solidarity
with those who need better housing, better public transit, and
better development that expresses a fundamental truth that no
matter what we use to get around—keys, farecard, or feet—we
are all welcome.

CHAPTER 4
COMMON GROUND, COMMON SEA

My first acting role was a small, but important one. It was a play about saving our planet, and I was a tree. I had no speaking lines, sure, but my green t-shirt and brown pants showed that audience of elementary school parents very clearly who I was. I stood there, swaying back and forth with the other trees, joining the rest of the third-grade cast in songs about doing our part to end pollution.

The 80s and 90s were a key time for raising awareness among youth to all kinds of issues. Both in and out of school we were taught how important it is to "reduce, reuse, recycle," a mantra filed side-by-side in our brains with others like "Be Smart, Don't Start," and "You could learn a lot from a dummy, buckle your safety belt." McGruff the Crime Dog would visit schools to teach kids how to say no to drugs, and Smokey the Bear reminded us often that preventing forest fires was up to us.

With all the issues to care about as a child, at least the environment seemed an easy cause to get behind. The county gave us a bright yellow bin to hold all those recyclable bottles next to our regular trash can, and a facility near our house actually paid us to bring them our empty aluminum cans. For a 10-year-old, exchanging trash for cash felt like a sweet deal. Nevermind that my brother and I would immediately go to the drugstore next door and spend all that cash on junk food. I would later come to learn that recycling our trash was merely the tip of the environmental iceberg.

It's at about this point when a few of my fellow Christians start to get uncomfortable. Some of us have been taught, either directly or indirectly, that caring about the planet is, as Jonathan Merritt put it bluntly, "for tree-hugging secularist liberals." Merritt's book, *Green Like God*, actually does a great job of making a biblical case for Christians to concern themselves with the state of creation. For now, though, I will try to summarize what he and others have discovered about the importance of what is sometimes called *creation care*.

But, first, a disclaimer. When I write about caring for the environment, let me be the first to tell you I don't have this all figured out. My wife and I have two cars, we haven't quite mastered the art of bringing reusable bags with us when we shop, and we aren't particularly stingy when it comes to cranking up the air conditioning when it's hot. Heck, I still have a couple incandescent light bulbs in my house. Sometimes recyclables end up in the trash, and sometimes the TV gets left on when no one's in the room. No one's perfect, right?

By the mere fact that God created earth, I believe we can all agree at a baseline that God cares about His creation. Genesis 1:31 says so: "Then God looked over all he had made, and he saw that it was very good!" Even before humans were here, in fact, God had the same reaction toward His creation, as shown earlier in verses 3, 10, 12, 18, and 25: "*it is good.*"

It is what we do with God's proclamation of Creation's goodness where we tend to diverge. For some, jumping on the "green" bandwagon means constantly looking for that new thing that will make us live more sustainable lives. Coffee mugs are labeled eco-friendly, not because they are made of recycled materials or are biodegradable, but because they are refillable. Cars are given the green moniker because the foam in the car's seats are made of plant-based materials, not because the car runs on solar or wind energy. Even Apple considers itself one of the most sustainable corporations in the world, a company known for building technologies that are obsolete in a few years' time[1]. Similarly, going green can be seen as a source of pride, a means of bragging to friends and family about how much we're doing for the environment. In a sense, sustainability has become something to be purchased, not a lifestyle change to be made in favor of consuming less.

Others dismiss the issue of sustainability entirely, claiming that environmentalism should not be a concern to Christians or, worse, that the impacts we are making on this planet aren't real. Even some well-known pastors have used their pulpit to speak out against the need for environmental stewardship. The Cornwall Declaration, written in 2000 and signed by many prominent faith leaders, claims, for instance, that environmental stewardship directly opposes economic progress, and that the threat of species loss are "of concern mainly to environmentalists in wealthy nations."[2] The document emphasizes laissez-faire government and accuses others of believing that "liberty, science, and technology are more a threat to the environment than a blessing to humanity and nature." The Cornwall Alliance's corresponding petition is boldly titled, "Forget 'Climate Change', Energy Empowers the Poor!," implying that those in support of climate science's findings are both anti-energy and lax on ending global poverty. Interestingly, though, the organization's core beliefs aren't anti-environment themselves, leading me to

believe that groups like Cornwall Alliance and the Southern
Baptist Environment & Climate Initiative, a coalition of faith
leaders decidedly more focused on addressing the damage done
to the environment by people, are more like ships in the night
than boxers in a ring[3]. As both groups purport to love God and
neighbor, perhaps there is common ground to be found.

The rest of us might simply be confused, unsure what to do
about the environment. We know recycling is a good thing to
do, and we know that sitting in bumper-to-bumper traffic can't
be good for the air, but beyond that we are paralyzed. Besides,
don't Christians have more important things to worry about, like
evangelism?

I think it is important to step back here and broadly define
what climate scientists are saying about our planet in order to
avoid basing our convictions on either doomsday predictions
about the earth's destruction or outright hostility toward any
concerted environmental protection efforts. Climatologists' foremost conclusion is that the increase in global temperatures has
accelerated over the past 40 years, largely as a result of increasing
carbon dioxide in the atmosphere[4]. Five of the warmest years
on record occurred from 2014 to 2018 (the most recent data
available at the time of this writing)[5]. And, the consensus is that
warming will continue[6].

Another key finding by scientists is that of rising sea levels.
Attributed to both the expansion of ocean waters as it warms
and the melting of Arctic and Antarctic ice, global sea levels have
increased by about 6.7 inches over the past century, and about
3.2 inches just since 1993, the start of when sea levels could be
observed by satellite[7]. America's East Coast is reported to have
experienced even higher levels of sea rise than other parts of
the U.S., with scientists discovering sea level rise as extreme as

one inch per year along the southeastern coast[8]. One nonprofit organization predicts that large swaths of major cities including Osaka, Shanghai, and Miami, could be permanently underwater if global temperatures rise by another 3 degrees Celsius[9].

Katharine Hayhoe is a climate scientist and professor at Texas Tech University, and she also happens to be a Christian and wife of a pastor. *Christianity Today* named her one of the 50 Women to Watch in 2012, and she made *TIME*'s 100 Most Influential People list in 2014[10]. Hayhoe says that research shows us more than 26,500 indicators that point to a warming climate, even when you account for the natural long-term cycles of the sun[11]. Based on long-term cycles, she reports, our planet was headed toward another Ice Age—a process that takes thousands of years—until we began burning oil and coal at increasing rates at the start of the Industrial Revolution. And, as it turns out, we have known that burning gases warms our planet since the Irish physicist John Tyndall first discovered it more than 150 years ago[12]. "It really *is* us this time," Hayhoe says.

Even though the majority of Americans either believe that climate change is due to human activities or that it might be due to a combination of human and natural causes, the effects on the climate can seem invisible to most of us. "Environmentally speaking, our heads are in the clouds," Jonathan Merritt writes[13].

> "We look around our suburban fortresses and see no devastation...Because we have been so financially blessed, most of us purchase the things we want, use them for awhile, and then throw them away without worrying about where they'll end up...Unfortunately, our solace is like drinking rum in a snowstorm. We feel warm, but the warmth isn't real."

Changes in average temperature of a couple degrees or sea level rises of a couple inches are imperceptible to our eyes or skin; thus, it's easy to be skeptical or doubt entirely what science has revealed. We see snow on the winter's ground and wonder aloud how it's possible the earth could be warming.

As a result, the issue of climate change has been left to battle it out in the political sphere, a few believing that environmental stewardship is a left-right issue rather than a scientific one. What may be missing from these arguments, however, is clear discussion on how alternatives to the status quo may actually be better for our families and for our children by improving our health, saving us money, and creating a long stream of new higher-wage jobs.

Health

The first reason tackling climate change is good for us is that it improves our health.

The World Health Organization estimates that about 235 million people suffer from asthma around the globe, and is considered the most prevalent chronic disease in children[14]. It is also on the rise: in 1980, about 3.6 percent of U.S. children had an asthma diagnosis[15]; as of 2017, the rate had jumped to 8.4 percent[16]. Nearly 8 percent of adults suffer from asthma, myself included. While some researchers had posited that a reason for the sudden increase in asthma prevalence was that society had gotten too hygienic, more robust data fails to support that hypothesis[17]. Although understanding asthma remains a challenge for the medical field, researchers agree that cleaning up the air that we and our children breathe is paramount in reducing asthma attacks.

While many of us picture factories spewing clouds of toxic

smoke into the atmosphere as our key source of poor air quality, the vehicles on our roadways are the largest source of pollution, accounting for 29 percent of all U.S. emissions[18]. Targeting those emissions, especially in congested areas, by reducing ozone and particulates generated by vehicle traffic can have immediate benefits in reducing asthma incidents and other respiratory problems. A study in Washington state found, for example, that school bus riders with asthma had reduced markers for lung inflammation after EPA standards were implemented that required school buses to swap diesel fuel with an ultra low sulfur diesel[19].

Not only are our lungs better off when we improve air quality, our hearts benefit as well. Research suggests our risk for cardiovascular disease is lowered when we take steps to reduce pollution generated by traffic[20]. Public health experts conclude that expanding public transportation networks and implementing strategies to reduce vehicle use in congested areas can significantly improve asthma and other public health outcomes[21].

Money

Secondly, rather than stifle our economy, addressing climate change can save us money.

Most of us know how widely the price of gas can swing. In the summer of 2008, the price at the pump peaked at a U.S. average of $4.11 per gallon, according to AAA[22]. Today, the price of gas has fallen back (for now), encouraging us to use more fuel and buy larger vehicles. Even still, each driver can expect to spend more than $1,300 a year fueling up their vehicle at today's gas prices, atop all the other costs of owning a car[23]. If you drive a large SUV or pickup truck, you're probably spending a lot more.

But what if you could skip the pump altogether? What if, instead of pumping our vehicles with dirty fuels and burning toxic coal to power our homes and businesses, we power our homes and cars in ways that don't cost us extra money while also protecting air and water quality for our children and grand-children? For example, solar power has traditionally been seen as a luxury too expensive for the average person. In 1975, the average cost for photovoltaic (PV) solar panels was more than 200 times higher than it is today[24]. In fact, the cost of solar has fallen about 70 percent just since 2010, putting small-scale systems (read: rooftop installations) more in reach for Americans[25]. Most estimates claim that PV panels will continue to fall in price into the future, albeit less drastically. And the savings from solar? On average, the savings from switching to solar power can pay back the cost of a system in about eight years[26], not to mention homes with solar tend to fetch a higher resale price than homes without[27].

Advances are also being made in the automotive industry. While the greenest cars are the ones not driven, electric vehicle technology has improved greatly, with better batteries being developed right now. As with solar, battery costs have been falling, which *Forbes* says will put electric vehicles in direct cost competition with gas-powered cars within the next decade[28]. While all-electric cars like the Nissan Leaf were initially released with a driving range of about 80 miles, newer models can go much further on a single charge. The Hyundai Kona Electric, released in 2019, has a reported range of nearly 260 miles[29], and the newest Teslas can achieve more than 300 miles on a charge, competitive with many gas-powered cars[30].

Even less costly than owning an efficient vehicle is using other modes of transportation to get around. Sure, great transit systems aren't available everywhere in the U.S., but where they are an option, they cost considerably less than owning a car, not to mention transit use encourages more physical activity. A regional pass that gets you around the Dallas-Fort Worth Metroplex costs $192 per month[31]. Portland caps the monthly cost of using its rail system at $100[32]. A monthly pass in Boston is just $90[33].

Bicycles are another option for getting around at a deep discount compared to driving. Though cycling in the U.S. had been reserved for Lycra-clad road warriors for many years, commuting on two wheels has grown in popularity thanks to increasing public investment in safer bike lanes. Basic bicycles can be found cheap at discount and sporting goods stores, with upright Dutch-style models aimed at commuters costing several hundred dollars more and found only at specialty bike shops. E-assist bicycles add an electric motor to help you arrive at your destination without breaking a sweat, and are especially useful on cargo bicycles, which allow you to haul groceries, children, and even furniture without having to splurge on an SUV. Of course, if you want the use of a bicycle without the maintenance of one, bike share systems are available in many cities and cost around $100 for an annual membership.

Job Creation

Lastly, working to reverse the impacts of climate change can actually be a job creator rather than a job killer.

One of the great myths being perpetuated to fight against the development of clean energy is that it will hurt the economy and leave millions out of work. Thankfully, data has proven otherwise. Employment in the American solar industry has grown 12 times faster than for all jobs[34], and today far more people work in the renewable energy sector than in oil and coal[35].

Globally, employment in renewable energy has increased as well. The International Renewable Energy Agency reports that total employment in clean energy increased from 5.7 million jobs in 2012 to 11 million jobs in 2018, the highest share of jobs being in solar, liquid biofuel, and wind energies[36, 37]. About 8 percent of those jobs are here in the United States.

———

I have a very fragile relationship when it comes to water. One of my recurring dreams involves crossing a bridge, only to find that I can't return because the tide has completely covered it with water. In real life, crossing the 4.5-mile Chesapeake Bay Bridge has always caused me to breathe a little heavier than normal. I have experienced water leaks or floods in nearly every place I've lived (and as I've said before, I have lived in a lot of places). In one house, our basement flooded after a weekend of non-stop rain, forcing us to throw away personal belongings we had kept there. In another, the water supply line to our refrigerator snapped, filling our second floor kitchen with water and spilling it through the front of the house onto the driveway. Where my wife and I now live, construction debris blocked our main drain, flooding our brand new house the night we moved in. Let's just say I'm pretty outspoken in favor of concrete floors.

Yet, the problems I've experienced with water are nothing compared to the damage water *can* do. We can turn on the news almost anytime and learn about another city wrecked by flood waters, whether an American city with the means to rebuild, or a city in a poorer nation where floods literally sweep away everything the people have. While these disasters are nothing new, scientists anticipate flooding will get worse in future years.

How do we know? Here are a few factors to consider:

First, it's important to understand where rainwater actually goes. In a natural setting with plentiful trees and no pavement, half of the rainwater that falls soaks into the ground and another 40 percent is soaked into the trees and other vegetation, leaving just 10 percent of that rain to run off into creeks, rivers, and so on[38]. The more we cover over our land with driveways, parking lots, big box buildings, and sprawling houses, the harder it is for the earth to capture the water for us, instead filling our streets and buildings with it, eventually carrying our pollution into rivers and oceans. A one-acre parking lot experiences 16 times the stormwater runoff of a one-acre area that is left natural. Couple that with regions where it's already tough for the soil to absorb rainwater, and there you have a recipe for disaster.

Second, as I covered earlier, melting ice in both Antarctica and Greenland contributes to our rising sea levels, meaning that rainstorms are more likely to cause floods in coastal areas. Places like Annapolis and Baltimore, Maryland, are flooding more often than ever, even without heavy rainfall events[39]. Recovering from these ever-worsening floods is incredibly expensive, too. FEMA estimates the total economic impact of Superstorm Sandy at over $70 billion, a hurricane that impacted nearly half of the United States and wreaked havoc on the New York City area[40]. Puerto Rico alone is estimated to require nearly $140 billion to recover after Hurricane Maria battered the island in 2017[41].

Conversely, as flooding events from hurricanes and other storms become more severe, so do droughts. Increases in air and water temperatures speed up evaporation, drying our ground of much-needed moisture. The effects of droughts are far-reaching, most importantly being the reduction and loss of food crops. Prolonged droughts also impact livestock, as some starve due to lack of food or as farmers are forced to sell off livestock to keep their livelihoods intact. In the U.S. alone, an estimated $9 billion is lost each year due to droughts[42].

Speaking of land and crops, the situation is also a bit fragile in this regard. Jonathan Merritt tells us that nearly 1,400 square miles of land—three times the land area of Los Angeles—become deserts each year, much of it affecting vulnerable populations in Africa[43]. The World Wildlife Fund reports that natural forests are being cut down at the rate of 48 football fields per minute, and that deforestation contributes about 15 percent of our greenhouse gas emissions[44]. Close to one-fifth of the Amazon rainforest has been lost in the past 50 years, and recent wildfires there have caused considerable damage to what's left[45]. If we now know that trees help capture rainfall, just imagine what happens when it rains but there are no longer any trees.

As carbon dioxide levels increase, crops are affected by nutrient loss. The EPA states, for example, that protein in soybeans decreases as CO_2 increases[46]. One major study involving researchers from across the globe indicates that rising CO_2 levels were associated with low iron and zinc content in wheat, rice, and corn, contributing to nutrient deficiencies in poorer nations like Bangladesh and Algeria[47]. The yield of commodity crops here in the U.S. are likely to be severely impacted by increasing CO_2 levels coupled with rising night time temperatures and more frequent extreme weather events[48]. Researchers from Canada and the U.K. discovered that droughts and heat waves have affected rice, wheat, and corn yields by roughly 10 percent in North America, Europe, and Australia, and predict that losses will worsen if climate projections continue to prove accurate[49].

—

There is good news hiding among all of these statistics, though. If human behavior does, in fact, have the capacity to accelerate climate change, we also have the capacity to slow it down. Deforestation has slowed around the world, as more countries are beginning to protect their forests from private interests[50]. Both the NOAA and the European Commission report that the number of marine species overfished has been declining[51, 52]. Researchers from Yale University and the University of California, Berkeley, found a 60 percent drop in emissions from manufacturing in the U.S. from 1990 to 2008, in spite of an increase in output[53]. Companies are discovering ways to turn trash into treasure, quite literally. Mars, Inc., the food corporation best known for making M&Ms and Skittles, announced in 2016 that it was able to divert all of its waste from landfills at each of its 126 global factories[54]. Here in San Antonio, Texas, one company has partnered with a cement manufacturer to capture 168 million pounds of its emissions each year and convert the byproduct into baking soda and other manufacturing chemicals[55].

Entrepreneurs across the globe are using their ingenuity to help mitigate the effects of our changing climate. Some examples of these businesses include:

- Azuri PayGo Energy, a program in 12 Sub-Saharan African countries that allows residents to power their homes with a solar panel that is paid for in increments much like a prepaid mobile phone[56].
- Fairphone, a Netherlands-based tech company that has designed an open-source smartphone that is easily repairable, uses less hazardous materials than typical phones, provides good working conditions to suppliers, and encourages recycling[57].

- Greenscape, an e-waste recovery and diversion
  company based in India that keeps unwanted
  electronics out of landfills by harvesting their com-
  ponents for reuse while also protecting amateur
  recyclers from toxic materials found in discarded
  electronics[58].

As individuals there are also several things we can do right
now to offer ourselves and our children a cleaner, brighter future.
Some of them are likely things you've heard many times before,
like unplugging appliances that aren't being used, switching
incandescent light bulbs to LEDs, and installing a program-
mable thermostat in your home. Some electricity providers will
even help with the cost of switching out your thermostat. Of
course, installing solar panels on your home is another great
way to cut electric bills and switch to a safer energy source. Yet,
even if you can't have panels installed where you live, you may
be able to choose an electricity provider that uses clean energy
like wind or solar. The choice to "green" your transportation is
also an important one, and could include switching to an electric
vehicle (especially if you charge it with those new solar panels),
swapping some of your vehicle trips with transit or bicycle trips,
and walking more for those around-the-corner trips to the store.

Other earth-friendly solutions are perhaps less obvious.
With livestock like cows, pigs, and chickens being significant
contributors to carbon emissions, adding more meatless meals
to your diet each week helps reduce our impact on the climate.
Believe it or not, even vegetables shipped from across the globe
are still better on the planet than locally-sourced red meat[59].
Washing clothes in cold water also makes a difference, not to
mention most modern detergents are just as effective at cleaning

your laundry in cold water as in hot water[60]. And cutting back on our use of plastics makes a dent, too, because plastic comes from the same raw material that's refined to fill your gas tank. Cutting out single-use plastic bags, for example, saves our storm drains as well as the hundreds of marine species that get trapped in the bags that wash into our rivers and oceans.

Churches certainly also have an important role to play when it comes to being good stewards of our planet. When I asked Katharine Hayhoe about this at an event, she suggested that churches first focus on efforts that will save them money[61]. "One of the things you can do in a church is an energy audit to figure out where money is being wasted, and get people involved in doing things to save money," she said. "Churches are a great way to actually model these things to people because you have a large group of people who share an enormous amount in common."

From there, Hayhoe encourages churches to take action beyond their walls. "The other thing is that climate change is a justice issue. Just like air pollution [and] water pollution, climate change disproportionately affects the poor. It happens here as well as on the other side of the world. When churches take these issues seriously, it is a witness like none other. You can say you care, but what really matters is what you do."

I am grateful to learn and report that churches across the nation are, in fact, taking environmental stewardship seriously. Many of the examples a church can set for its congregation are similar to what families can be doing at home, like recycling waste, exchanging some of its disposable materials like foam cups for reusable ones, adding sensors that turn off lights when no one's in the room, and replacing thirsty turf grasses with low-water landscaping. First Congregational Church in Atlanta made several changes to its historic property, replacing 32 parking spaces with a garden, switching to low-water plumbing fixtures, and encouraging attendees to use public transit to attend services. Christ United Methodist Church in Plano, Texas offers bicycle parking and recycled much of the construction waste created while building its large sanctuary. A small congregation in Wayne County, Ohio used recycled materials when constructing its building while also adding a rainwater collection system that is used to flush its toilets. Florida Avenue Baptist Church in Washington, D.C. covered its century-old roof in solar panels. And, a Jewish center in Philadelphia has started a campaign encouraging its families to move their financial investments away from fossil fuels and into clean energy, including steps like using local banks and credit unions that do not invest in oil or coal-related corporations as well as moving long-term investments away from companies that contribute to pollution.

For years environmental groups have taken the lead on caring for God's creation, while we as Christians have either opted out of the conversation altogether or assimilated the positions held by the political parties we support. Yet, when we pause to consider God's heart, we learn that He does, in fact, care about how we treat the planet. We learn in Psalm 19:1 that Creation is a reflection of God's glory. Job 37 describes God's creativity in forming our planet. We are told in Ezekiel 34 that caring only for ourselves and not the rest of His creation is a big problem:

"Woe to you shepherds of Israel who only take care of yourselves! Should not shepherds take care of the flock? You eat the curds, clothe yourselves with the wool and slaughter the choice animals, but you do not take care of the flock." (Ezekiel 34:2-3)

Taking care of our flocks—and the pastures on which they graze—is no easy task. And, while some churches have grown to become shining examples of God's love for people and planet, others have yet to fully seize this opportunity, as we will see in the next chapter.

CHAPTER 5
HERE COMES THE CHURCH

I still remember the harvest green van, with its rows of camel-colored vinyl bench seats. I remember our driver, who was also one of the youth pastors: a tall, older man with a thin, white crew cut and black-rimmed glasses. Other than his age and hair color, I could tell that not much had changed about him since he fought in the Korean War. The old van would pick up my brother and me each week for Sunday School, bringing us to the classic brick church building, complete with white steeple and clear-stained oak pews. I remember the bright red carpet that blanketed the sanctuary, the flower-shaped butter cookies and fruit punch we would get as kids during services, and the sound system that played instrumental cassettes of Southern Gospel songs sung by a row of bushy-haired women in matching red choir robes. My fondest memories of that church were playing in the handbell choir, clad in the same red polyester robes (yes, I can see the cool points racking up here).

The church my wife and I attended in Austin was altogether different. There was no van, no pews, no choir robes, no bushy-haired ladies, and the cheap cookies were replaced with fair-trade coffee. Heck, there wasn't even a building. While our church had multiple campuses, we met in schools rather than in dedicated

buildings, with scores of volunteers setting up its weekly operation in the gymnasium. Our campus operation spilled out into
the high-school hallway, completing the experience with plush
lounge areas and even a bookstore. In the sanctinasium was a
fairly elaborate stage with screens that could be seen by weekly
attendees seated in the bleachers, probably 50 rows back. The
worship leader was a gifted man, even though his tattoo-covered
arms and skinny jeans would probably give my old church's
ladies a heart attack.

This is just a sampling of the churches I've been part of in
my life. Some have had pews, others had a previous life as a tire
shop or grocery store. Some were small enough that everyone's
business was out in the open, others so large you could attend
for years and go completely unnoticed. There are more than
300,000 churches in America, by some estimates, so there are
bound to be nearly as many ways to "do church." And, while my
point in this chapter is not to point out that some are doing things
right and others wrong, I do believe that the modern American
church has adapted to our way of building over the past century,
which has led to a host of consequences I hope to address here.

The earliest churches weren't meeting in awe-inspiring
cathedrals in historic city centers or purpose-built auditoriums
on the edges of town. Christians were worshiping in public
spaces and in people's homes and, in some cases, borrowed
spaces*. In fact, the first building believed to be dedicated for
use by Christians was renovated roughly 200 years after Jesus'
death and resurrection[1]. Even then, the building, located in what
is now Syria, was destroyed shortly thereafter. Archaeologists
believe the first building constructed specifically as a church is

---

*See Acts 2:46, Acts 12:12, Acts 19:9, Acts 20:7-8, Colossians 4:15, and 1
Corinthians 16:19

the Aqaba Church in Jordan, dated around 300 A.D. When first built, it could only accommodate about 60 people, according to one article[2].

At about the same time the Aqaba Church was completed more than 700 miles away, construction began on what is now considered the oldest cathedral in the world, the Etchmiadzin Cathedral in western Armenia. Though there is some debate as to how elaborate the original structure was, what remains is considered an important piece of Christian history and is designated a UNESCO World Heritage Site.

For me, one of the most uniquely amazing church buildings I've ever visited was St. Nicholas' Church in Wismar, Germany. Completed in the 1400s on Germany's northern coast, I was struck not only by the sheer mass of this red brick building, at more than 120 feet tall, but also the fact that most of its Gothic structure and interior are original, having survived the destruction of World War II that befell much of the region. Its flying buttresses that surround the apse seem to defy gravity, and is most impressive considering that this was all built without modern technology. While most of what is built in America today barely survives a half-century, even the murals inside St. Nicholas' Church remain intact.

Of course, none of these early churches compare to what is, by far, the largest purpose-built church in the world, St. Peter's Basilica in Vatican City. The Renaissance-style church was completed in 1626, more than 120 years after groundbreaking, and has an interior measuring 163,000 square feet, which is three times the size of the White House[3, 4]. It is a design marvel, even 400 years later, with its interior covered in what looks like more than a hundred paintings but are, in fact, painstakingly intricate mosaics covering an area the equivalent of 7 NBA basketball courts.

The largest church in America wasn't actually built to be a church. Known first as The Summit, and later as Compaq center, Joel Osteen's Lakewood Church hosted the Houston Rockets from the time it opened in 1975 until 2003, when the team moved to its new home in downtown Houston[5]. Lakewood began leasing the stadium from the City of Houston in 2003, investing $95 million to retrofit the space for its worship services. It opened in 2005 and seats 16,000 people. According to a 2016 estimate, Lakewood is attended by about 52,000 people each week[6], and millions more watch Osteen's services on television and streaming services.

Megachurches like Lakewood seem to be sprouting up with increasing frequency. While large churches have existed for centuries, the media began distinguishing them from other congregations in the 1980s. Dave Travis and Scott Thumma, in their 2007 book *Beyond Megachurch Myths*, estimate that only about 50 American megachurches existed in 1970, having congregations of 1,500 or more people. Today well over 1,600 churches fit the definition[7].

Living in Texas, I have visited my fair share of megachurches. Here in San Antonio is one of the largest in the state, Community Bible Church, which has a weekly attendance of about 14,000 people[8]. Its sprawling campus covers 52 acres, more than twice the land area of a typical Walmart Supercenter, and includes two auditoriums, two cafes, a child care wing, and a store. And while its lobby may look more like a convention center than a worship center, CBC also provides dozens of opportunities to do local outreach and international missions. According to the church's website, one can volunteer by serving food or delivering blankets to the homeless, contribute diapers to the Texas Diaper Bank, or serve on short-term teams in countries like Guatemala, Kenya, and Nepal[9]. There are also more than 250 groups that meet throughout the week, offering opportunities to build community and study the bible, with some serving specific needs like a bible study for people with autism and other intellectual disabilities.

With so many churches across the country, ranging in size from those meeting in one's living room to those filling a stadium, it's tempting to ask the question, which model is best? Are small churches best or do big churches do it better? The short answer is: *it depends*.

As I discussed in Chapter 2, parking is one issue that seems to get many people fired up. If I had the chance to ask you, I'd bet you could tell me an absurd story about the ways we behave in parking lots. The viral rap video, "It's Getting Real in the Whole Foods Parking Lot," parodies the tension of waiting for a parking space to open up, and Tyler Perry characterized in the 2009 movie *Madea Goes to Jail* just how explosive we can be when others "steal" our parking space. Sadly these tensions can be no less ridiculous in real life, nor are churches exempt from them. Neighborhoods routinely battle with churches over the provision of parking for its parishioners, pastors hoping to accommodate growing congregations and residents looking to keep their community fabric intact. One church in a Chicago suburb, for example, battled with neighborhood residents for years over its plans to demolish eight homes to build a surface parking lot, but dropped the idea in 2013 when leaders decided instead to use two nearby school parking lots and shuttle congregants to its campus[10]. A Memphis-based church sat at odds with its neighbors over the possible demolition of a historic home that would have been replaced with parking and an expanded soccer field[11]. As of this writing, demolition has not occurred.

Neighborhood residents also show no shortage of outrage when nearby churches attempt to expand their buildings. One church in Clifton Park, New York struggled to get support to replace its existing building because it would, as the *Albany Times Union* reported, "turn their quiet neighborhood into a busy, chaotic tangle of cars."[12] Third Church near Richmond, Virginia also met intense opposition when it originally planned its expansion in the mid-2000s.

When tensions like these arise, it is no surprise, then, that American churches have spent decades fleeing neighborhoods altogether. Across the nation, church leaders are choosing to locate their facilities along freeways, on city edges, and in other nonresidential areas to host their weekly services, trading local community for cheap dirt. Certainly it is the case here in the South, where countless churches are accessible only by car, parking lots completely disconnected from adjacent residents. There is even a whole selection of resources for churches on "parking lot ministry," advising churches how to deal with the throngs of drivers who, no doubt, battle other church-goers for road space on the way to their worship services.

Churches, of course, feel a duty to serve its congregants, to provide a welcoming environment where attendees return week after week to be encouraged and challenged by the Word of God. Practically speaking, this is accomplished first and foremost by making space for them. Installing chairs or pews. Giving access to parking, either on- or off-site. Providing transportation for those who can't get to church on their own. But, as churches grow in size, meeting these practical needs becomes increasingly difficult. Since I first walked into Pearl Street Church nearly five years ago, weekly attendance has quadrupled, straining our ability to provide both parking and seating. Its bustling location at the edge of downtown adds to our challenges: our dedicated parking lot is being replaced with a 10-story mixed-use office building, forcing us to reconsider how we can accommodate everyone who wants to be there.

Yet, serving our neighbors is also a critical call for churches. When Jesus commanded us to love our neighbors, I propose that He would apply this to our institutions as well. This means doing all the things that make us good neighbors, like cleaning up our trash, keeping our landscaping neat, and not having loud parties. It means learning who our neighbors are, whether residents or business owners, finding ways to meet their practical needs. It means throwing parties for our neighbors with no other agenda than to know them better. And, when conflict arises, it means choosing listening over litigation. Compromise over confrontation.

Being a compassionate congregation can be tough when church members do not live in the neighborhood where the church is located. More often than not, hundreds pour into parking lots on Sunday (or Saturday) mornings, store their cars while they worship, and then head out to their favorite lunch spot before driving back home. I get it. I have never personally lived in the same neighborhood where my church is planted. In fact, more than half of the churches I called home were large and struggled with accommodating all the people arriving from across town. Some had fallen into the trap of becoming highway churches. Yet, one church in particular has always stood out to me as one that successfully manages the delicate balance of loving neighbors and serving its diverse congregation.

When Antioch Community Church moved into north-central Waco, Texas, in 2000, the neighborhood was a difficult place to be, riddled with drugs and prostitution. Poverty was high and the local grocery store had fled the scene, leaving a building behind that would soon house Antioch's growing congregation. Attendees would undoubtedly drive in from other parts of the city to worship, but that did not stop Antioch's leadership from making a radical decision that would come to transform the neighborhood. Many of the pastors decided that they could best love the neighborhood their church would call home if their families, too, called the neighborhood home. One by one, they moved into Sanger-Heights and, through intentional relation-ship-building, developed deep trust with long-time residents. The church also established residential facilities to free the men and women in the neighborhood gripped by addiction, rather than just push them out. By the time Antioch sought to expand its building a decade later (debt-free, by the way), other local churches' members had begun moving into the neighborhood as well. By 2011, the nonprofit Waco Community Development Corporation reported that roughly one-third of their homebuy-ers were members of a local church, including Antioch[13].

One of the key ways that churches like Antioch serve neigh-borhoods well is by meeting together in them. Much in the same way early churches met in people's homes, small groups gather together between weekly services to study scripture, share meals, and pray for one another. To readers who have not been part of a church, the idea of showing up to a stranger's house and reading and praying together in a circle might seem strange. Cultish, even. I would argue, however, that small groups serve not only to make larger churches more accessible to people who struggle to connect with others, they also create a space that fosters encouragement and spiritual discipline among one another. When done well, they can transform people's lives. In *Community 101*, Gilbert Bilezikian writes:

"It is in small groups that people can get close enough to know each other, to care and share, to challenge and support, to confide and confess, to forgive and be forgiven, to laugh and weep together, to be accountable to each other, to watch over each other and to grow together. Personal growth does not happen in isolation. It is the result of interactive relationships. Small groups are God's gift to foster changes in character and spiritual growth."[14]

Small groups from Antioch Community Church, known as Lifegroups, routinely sought ways not just to build relationships among each other, but to serve the broader community. Leaders helped gather volunteers to care for a neighbor's yard, while a heart for those struggling with poverty led to a weekly dinner celebration called The Feast. In the church where my wife and I now serve, John and Teri rally dozens of volunteers to serve local ministries focused on helping those in need. And on the weeks when they're not volunteering, John and Teri host volunteers in their home to share a meal and talk about life.

I have personally been part of more than a dozen different small groups over the years, starting with a group in high school that wasn't even a small group in the official sense. The groups ranged in type and size, some open only to guys, others co-ed. Some were attended by only a handful of people, others so large we'd jokingly call them "medium groups." To say that these groups have impacted my life would be an understatement. It is because of small groups that I learned it's okay for guys to share their struggles with one another, and that vulnerability leads to maturity. It was in a small group that I found my wife. And, it is because of small groups that we are still married today, with a marriage that grows healthier all the time.

Saddleback Church is often considered a success story when it comes to small group ministry, in part because of this fact: more people meet in Saddleback small groups each week than actually attend their church services[15]. A seemingly impossible statistic, this didn't happen by accident. Brett Eastman recalls that when he arrived at Saddleback, only 700 people were attending weekly small groups, despite a church that was home to more than 15,000[16]. Getting from less than five percent participation to 100 percent participation would be a challenge, but one that both Eastman and senior pastor Rick Warren were committed to. In the wake of what has become one of the best-selling books ever written, *The Purpose-Driven Life*, Saddleback's emphasis on small groups had resulted in more than 20,000 people meeting weekly in homes across southern California.

The time Jesus spent with His 12 disciples was filled with many of the same principles we see in modern small groups. They challenged one another, they shared meals together, and they prayed for each other. But more importantly, out of what they gained together they poured into their community. In Matthew 28, Jesus told the disciples something vital that continues to shape Christian ministry to this day: "Go and make disciples of all the nations, baptizing them in the name of the Father and the Son and the Holy Spirit. Teach these new disciples to obey all the commands I have given you." For those of you who have attended church for any length of time, you've probably heard sermons dissecting this passage, known broadly as The Great Commission. Some interpret this scripture as a discrete command to evangelism. International missions organizations inevitably focus on "all the nations," using this verse to recruit volunteers to their work in foreign countries. Yet, while evangelism and world missions are both vital to the Christian faith, what Jesus was telling the men was to replicate what He did with them. Perhaps a modern translation of these verses could say, "As you go through life together, here and abroad, be intentional with your neighbors, modeling my way of love for them, to the point that they would develop and model that same love for others." And isn't that the point of the Church, to intentionally model the experiential and unconditional love of God for others? After all, by modeling a true reflection of His love, would people not be attracted to it?

So, if I go back to my first question here in this chapter, the answer is not that big churches are better than small ones, or small churches better than big ones. It's not about the green van or the red choir robes, the fog machines or the dynamic preaching. It's not about having a state-of-the-art sanctinasium or a parking lot ministry. Rather, it is more important that churches foster Jesus' definition of community, enabling people to engage with others in love, share life together, spur each other on, and inspire others to do the same with their neighbors. It's called making disciples.

In the context of city building, I want to highlight a few ways that churches are fostering community in their own neighborhoods:

The Church as Developer

In response to the growing affordable housing crisis in Colorado, Denver-based architecture firm Radian teamed up with the Interfaith Alliance of Colorado to create the Congregation Land Campaign as a way to help churches in the Denver region turn their estimated 5,000 acres of vacant land into housing for lower-income families. Since most church leaders lack expertise in real estate development, the Congregation Land Campaign team offers guidance throughout the process, ensuring that what gets built benefits the community at large. Since then, CLC has partnered with churches throughout Colorado to create housing opportunities for local residents, and currently has six projects in the pipeline that will result in more than 160 new homes.

The Church as Third Place

Urban sociologist Ray Oldenburg famously coined the term "third place" to describe where people spend time outside of home and work. These are essentially community gathering spaces that include cafes, parks, libraries, and other spots where people can come together freely for conversation regardless of socioeconomic status. Churches that are rooted in a local neighborhood can serve as third places, opening their doors beyond weekend services for day-to-day gatherings as well as community events. The Camp House, an outgrowth of Mission Chattanooga, is an example of this kind of third place, one that director and pastor Matt Busby said in *Christianity Today* was designed to "foster community and cultivate culture in our city."[17] While The Camp House serves as a coffee shop in downtown Chattanooga, Tennessee, throughout the week, the space is outfitted for church services on Sunday. Busby says that The Camp House is not an add-on ministry of Mission Chattanooga, but rather sees the daily use of the space as "faithful stewardship" of their prime location in the city.

The Church as Compassionate Neighbor

For my last example, let's return to the story of Third Church near Richmond, Virginia. As I mentioned earlier, the church leadership had faced great opposition from the surrounding neighborhood when it had planned a campus expansion during the mid-2000s. Third Church has a fairly large congregation of more than 1,200 members and felt they needed to build additional parking and square footage to accommodate them all. The lack of process at that time created a chasm between the church and the neighborhood, something that struck Corey Widmer, the man who would later become the church's head pastor.

Andrew Moore, an architect and trustee at Third Church, came to Widmer close to a decade later with the question, "what does it mean for Third Church to be an expression of the Kingdom of God in the physical environment?" That question ultimately led to a multi-day workshop filled with ideas and sketching (known as a charrette), enlisting neighbors, nearby business owners, church members, and students from Judson University to think holistically about how to improve not just the church itself but the area surrounding it.

Moore and a team of volunteers led the charrette in early 2017, gathering ideas, studying how people travel along the corridor, and sketching everything from courtyards to crosswalks. The team met with church staff and neighbors, they walked around the vicinity, they spoke with business owners from the shopping center located across the street, and even engaged the school district to test whether they could help with the nearby elementary school's bus traffic issues.

Ultimately, Widmer's goal was that neighbors would see Third Church as a vital part of the neighborhood, even if neighbors didn't happen to share the same theology. He said that the measure of success for the church isn't just about how well it serves its members but, "by how we're contributing to the flourishing of the surrounding community." In *Generous Justice*, Timothy Keller says, "When a city perceives a church as existing strictly and only for itself and its own members, the preaching of that church will not resonate with outsiders. But if neighbors see church members loving their city through astonishing, sacrificial deeds of compassion, they will be much more open to the church's message."

It is that message that inspired Widmer to lead the church in redefining its vision statement in a way that, I believe, really captures the vision of the broader church: "Called together for the renewal of all things through Jesus Christ."[18]

CHAPTER 6
JUSTICE

The little boy bullied on the playground. The woman beaten by her drunken husband. The man denied service because of the color of his skin. An innocent bystander killed in a drive-by shooting. We all claim to know injustice when we see it—the good made victim through no fault of their own. And, in this regard, most of us can say we know what injustice feels like.

"You better not walk home from school," he told me, his voice uncompromising in his threat to make sure I understood how different I was from the rest of the kids. At 10 years old, I learned well what it was to be teased, mocked for walking and talking differently than the other boys. But, this was the first time I was to be hit because of it. So, with equal parts humiliation and gratitude, a school counselor drove me home that day to avoid the spectacle I would've become.

Of course, a simple scan of any news cycle will reveal that the bullying I experienced 25 years ago has only gotten worse for other children since then. A disturbing number of children have needlessly taken their own lives in the midst of endless taunting by their peers: kids like Kenneth Weishuhn, Jr., who are bullied for their sexual orientation, and Hannah Smith, who are taunted by anonymous cyberbullies because of their appearance.

The rise in cyberbullying led to Texas passing what is known as "David's Law," legislation that empowers schools to take action against online bullying occurring off school property, written after 16-year-old David Molak committed suicide in 2016 following relentless online harassment and threats here in the San Antonio area[1]. Molak's brother said of the incident on Facebook, "In today's age, bullies don't push you into lockers, they don't tell their victims to meet them behind the school's dumpster after class, they cower behind usernames and fake profiles from miles away..."[2] Similar laws to end cyberbullying have been passed in California, Connecticut, and Oklahoma.

Yet, no conversation about injustice is complete without reflecting on the injustice that has been experienced by minority groups throughout history, and particularly American history. In the prior century alone, America's timeline is full of degrading and violent acts toward African Americans and other minorities. At the turn of the 20th Century, prominent politicians like Senator Benjamin Tillman from South Carolina advocated for legalizing the lynching of African Americans, a practice that had grown rampant across the southern half of the nation[3]. And, from the latter part of the 19th Century through about 1950, researchers estimate that about 4,000 blacks were killed in this manner, often with dozens, if not hundreds, of spectators[4].

Slavery, thought to be a primarily 19th Century phenomenon, persisted into the early 1900s. Although the Thirteenth Amendment was ratified at the end of 1865, a few states rejected the new law, including Delaware and Kentucky. In fact, Delaware did not formally abolish slavery until 1901[5]. Furthermore, as Douglas Blackmon reported in his book *Slavery by Another Name*, millions of African Americans were forced into labor with little to no wages, up until World War II.

Even today, racial injustice runs rampant across America. We see it in events like the 2015 church shooting in Charleston, South Carolina and the 2017 vehicle attack on protesters in Charlottesville, Virginia; yet, there are thousands of other events you and I have never heard about. While hate crimes have fallen dramatically over the past several decades, the Federal Bureau of Investigation reported that, in 2017 alone, there were over 2,000 hate crimes committed against African Americans in the U.S., far more than the numbers reported for any other people group[6]. The U.S. Equal Employment Opportunity Commission found more than 23,000 cases between 2000 and 2019 where racial discrimination was evident in employment decisions[7]. And, the National Fair Housing Alliance reported over 5,800 instances in 2018 where people of color were denied housing, steered toward minority neighborhoods, offered predatory mortgage loans, or otherwise treated unfairly because of their race[8].

Unfortunately, Christians in America have not had the best track record, either, when it comes to racial discrimination and other injustices. Noel Rae discusses in his book *The Great Stain* the ways in which Christian slaveholders in the U.S. used the Bible to defend chattel slavery. Yale professor of religious history Tisa Wenger highlights what she calls the weaponization of religious freedom. Even as slavery was outlawed and Christians' views toward it had softened, these views had been replaced by "segregationist folk theology that defended the reconstituted Southern racial order as divinely ordained: God had created the races separate and did not intend for them to mix."[9] Thus, attempts to end Jim Crow laws and promote integration through affirmative action were opposed by many prominent pastors and Christian leaders through the mid- and late-20th Century. In his groundbreaking book *The Color of Compromise*, Jemar Tisby documents the long history of the American Church's complicity in racism from the Colonial era through modern times.

While conditions have improved, still significant numbers of Christians demonstrate racially biased views. More than one in five white evangelicals say small businesses should be allowed to refuse service to African Americans on the basis of religious beliefs[10]. White evangelicals also believe more strongly than other groups that the U.S. criminal justice system is equally fair to blacks and whites, that police officers treat blacks and whites equally, and that the well-known police shootings of black men in cities like Ferguson, Missouri, and Baltimore, Maryland were isolated incidents[11]. In 2015, author Bradley Wright also found bias in how church members respond to emails by fictional people whose names fit a racial stereotype. In his study Wright found that some denominations were significantly less likely to respond to messages showing interest in their local church if they appeared to be sent by African Americans, Hispanics, or Asians than if they seemed to come from a white person[12]. In attempting to find an explanation for this implicit racial bias among white Christians, Wright wrote:

> "What matters to evangelicals is how you treat the person in front of you...From this perspective, racial discrimination is rooted in poor relationships and personal sin, not in systems of injustice perpetuated by the government, media, or education. It happens when individuals treat other individuals wrong."

As such, the majority of us might say that, when it comes to our personal relationships, we don't hold any hatred toward people of other races or harbor overtly racist tendencies. But, as Vincent Carpenter, Teaching Pastor at Antioch Community Church in Waco, Texas, says, "Racism does not express itself always through individual relationships. Often times, in our modern society, racism expresses itself through our systems and through our cultural structures."[13] Even though Bradley Wright recognizes that an "individualistic approach might lead evangelicals to distrust broader, societal-level programs for addressing racial inequality," Carpenter suggests that we are often complicit in racist outcomes even without racist intent. In a recent sermon, Carpenter goes on to give this example:

> "Let's say a company wants to hire an employee. . . .There could be 50 or 100 applications for a specific position. But typically, as opposed to just wading through lots of unknown applications, the manager will go to the employees of that same company and say, 'Hey, we need to fill this position...Who do you know that you can recommend?' And as those employees recommend people, those applications generally go to the top of the stack. Those applications at the top of the stack have a significantly higher opportunity to be interviewed and, subsequently, hired. If the managers are one particular race, say, Caucasian, and the employees are of the same race... and their network of relationships are people that are Caucasian...the outcome of that system has a racist [effect]."

Perhaps one key element to dealing with racial injustice among Christians is acknowledging that it exists. White Christians are, by and large, much less aware of discrimination against blacks than Americans as a whole[14]. Some groups and leaders are hoping their work will enlighten fellow Christians to the realities of racial injustice and inspire us all toward inclusivity. In the final chapter of *The Color of Compromise*, Jemar Tisby offers several practical ways in which American Christians and our churches can begin to stand against our nation's long history of racism. Repentance of racism, Tisby argues, means that white Christians will not only need to gain a better understanding of black history and theology, but will also need to partner with African Americans in ensuring racial justice is integrated into education, the arts, and politics.

Justice and the Built Environment

One often overlooked manifestation of injustice in our society has to do with where we live. Our built environment is a daily reminder that we prioritize some facets of humanity over others. Our streets, our homes, and the municipal services that support them, all speak to the realities facing our communities that all are not treated equitably. Researchers have found that life expectancy is highly correlated with ZIP codes, meaning that where you live could determine when you die[15].

Think about the last time you walked somewhere from your home or office or school. Consider that experience for a moment. When you stepped outside, was there a sidewalk available to you? Was it wide enough to pass another person comfortably? Was it in decent condition? Were there trees along the street and other greenery to look at?

Think about the traffic along your walk. How many lanes of traffic were there along that road? How many vehicles were driving by you as you walked? How fast were they driving? Was there a safe place for bicycles to also use that road? And, when you reached an intersection, how long did it take you to cross the street? Did you feel safe doing so?

Now, also think about your surroundings. What sorts of destinations were nearby? Were there any places you could go to meet a friend? To buy healthy foods? To play or get exercise? Could you catch a bus or train easily?

In many cities across North America, this exercise doesn't lead to very encouraging imagery. Many neighborhoods built during the middle and late 20th Century lack sidewalks. Many streets, and particularly those in high-poverty areas, lack trees[16]. Wide streets with fast-moving cars are prevalent throughout most of our cities, offering few places to cross safely as a pedestrian. Our landscapes are often dotted with destinations set far back from the road to give priority to cars, making it difficult to access them by foot. And, when the weather is foul, subpar stormwater systems mean that rainwater collects on street edges, ready to drench pedestrians as cars go by.

I realize that nobody woke up one morning and decided that people who walk are inferior human beings, even though evidence points to the automotive industry creating a concerted attack against pedestrians and transit systems in the 1920s and 30s[17, 18]. Instead, as our automobile culture grew rapidly throughout the mid-20th Century, accommodating people who walk, bike, or use transit became less and less of a priority. Cities divested from rail, builders omitted sidewalks from their new subdivisions to save money, and transportation departments focused their attention on moving cars faster. All of this in an effort to improve Americans' quality of life, leading to a host of ironic results.

In 1909, the year following the release of the Ford Model T, less than 1,200 people were killed in traffic crashes, or about

1.3 people per 100,000 population. By World War II, the death
rate had ballooned to more than 28 people per 100,000. Then,
by the late 1960s and throughout the 1970s, more than 50,000
people were dying annually on our roads. Safety measures like
seat belts, airbags, and improved vehicle designs have helped
bring that number down. Yet, as I mentioned in Chapter 3, more
than 30,000 people continue to die each year due to incidents
involving our vehicles, about 6,000 of those people being on
foot[19]. What's more, minorities are more likely to be killed while
walking than white people are[20].

Even if you manage to avoid being injured or killed in a
vehicle-related crash, living in neighborhoods built around the
automobile can be a health hazard in itself. Low density neighborhoods with disconnected streets and a lack of sidewalks are
associated with an increased risk of being overweight, says one
2006 study[21]. More recently, researchers from the University of
Connecticut and the University of Colorado set out to study why
that is. They discovered that communities with more intersec-
tions—that is, neighborhoods having more of a grid layout—
experience lower rates of obesity as well as heart disease, high
blood pressure, and diabetes. On the other hand, people living in
conventional suburbs—those neighborhoods with long, curved
streets, terminating in the cul-de-sac—spend significantly more
time behind the wheel, leading to poor health outcomes and an
increased chance of death in an automobile crash. More specifically, neighborhoods characterized by having big box stores are
associated with 25 percent higher rates of diabetes and nearly
14 percent higher rates of obesity than other neighborhoods[22].

Unfortunately, we are not often taught to consider the
connection between neighborhood design and our health when
deciding where to live, much less to demand better options from

our local officials. When my wife and I were shopping for our home nearly five years ago, our Realtor was surprised that I would not even consider looking at a home if it meant a transit commute of an hour or more. I guess few, if any, of her clients had ever made this a requirement in their house hunt.

Now, the fact that my wife and I had some choice in where we'd ultimately buy a home is something not many working class families enjoy. In cities across the U.S., families earning lower incomes are typically relegated to less desirable neighborhoods, with homes in deteriorating condition, poor access to healthy foods, and lower-performing public schools. That is, if they're able to buy a house at all.

According to mortgage expert Keith Gumbinger, the salary needed to buy a home in most major U.S. cities is increasingly out of reach for the typical family. In San Antonio, Texas, a salary of $64,000 would be required to purchase a median-priced home with a 10 percent down payment. In Chicago, a family needs to earn at least $73,000 a year. And, in San Francisco, it's a whopping $211,000[23]. With home prices rising faster than wages since the mid-1970s, there are no signs that the two will converge again in the future[24]. The picture is similarly bleak in Canada and the U.K.[25, 26]

But what does buying a home have to do with justice? After all, owning a home is considered a choice. The problem for those who *want* to buy lies with housing policy. Research continues to demonstrate that strict land use regulations, especially rules prohibiting attached or affordable housing construction, exacerbate wealth inequality and have led to a loss in housing wealth among the middle class[27]. In places where neighbors routinely lobby against new development and, more specifically, against lower-priced housing, families with more moderate incomes are

usually forced to rent or, alternatively, to buy in far exurban neighborhoods where regulations are less strict and commutes are far
longer. Meanwhile, neighborhoods close to city centers that for
decades have been home to predominantly poor and minority
households are seeing increased market interest, pushing some
of those long-time residents out into the suburbs as well.

Yet, renter households—and specifically lower-income
renter households—are in the most precarious position when it
comes to housing stability. Not only are lower-income renters
more likely to face evictions than other families, they are also
more likely to live in substandard conditions, all while spending a
much bigger portion of their earnings to stay there[28]. According
to Matthew Desmond, Harvard University professor and author
of the award-winning book *Evicted*, more than half of renter
households are cost burdened, meaning they spend at least one-
third of their income on housing expenses. Minority families
are even worse off, with one in four black and Hispanic renting
households spending at least half their income on housing.
Desmond points out that housing instability and evictions
lead to a host of problems including increased risk of job loss,
poor school performance in children, exposure to exploitative
housing conditions, depression, and loss of access to food and
basic medical care. In many ways we have stacked the deck, so to
speak, against our lower-income and minority families, creating
waves of vulnerability through their lives.

The Role of Compassion in Justice

The list of injustices we face in our society can seem endless,
which begs the question: why are people treated so unjustly
anyway? One factor that may explain the injustices present
in our built environment involves the word *compassion*, whose

original definition means "to suffer with." As it turns out, it is much harder to have compassion for people we don't know than for those we do.

Researchers from the University of California, Berkeley, discovered that it is actually the less affluent who demonstrate greater compassion than the wealthy[29]. Regardless of race, gender, or spiritual beliefs, those with more means actually tend to show more selfish behaviors than those with greater need. But, how can that be? Doesn't society tell us that people in poverty are more susceptible to greed and to accepting handouts than the middle and upper classes? Aren't *they* the ones more likely to steal?

A *Scientific American* article summarizes this research into one important statement: "The less we have to rely on others, the less we may care about their feelings."[30]

The implication of these findings is huge when it comes to where we live. As David Roberts wrote, "our ability to form and maintain friendships is shaped in crucial ways by the physical spaces in which we live."[31] The more we are behind the wheel, for instance, the less we interact directly with other human beings. We feel as though we are competing against other machines for road space and parking. Often times, the only thing we know about our neighbors in modern suburbs is what kind of car they drive.

In Chapter 2, I brought up the growing income segregation that exists across the country, and especially Sun Belt cities. The phenomenon shows that, not only do we tend to select neighborhoods that are racially similar to ourselves, we are increasingly more likely to live near people who earn as much as we do, stratifying our communities into pockets of economic sameness. As the *Scientific American* article reports, "If social class influences how much we care about others, then the most powerful among us may be the least likely to make decisions that help the needy and the poor." As Christians, this should be deeply concerning. The Scriptures are clear that an important component to enacting justice is making decisions that help the poor.

We see it in James 1:27: "Pure and genuine religion in the sight of God the Father means caring for orphans and widows in their distress and refusing to let the world corrupt you."

We can also find it in the Old Testament: "Learn to do good. Seek justice. Help the oppressed. Defend the cause of orphans. Fight for the rights of widows." (Isaiah 1:17)

"...This is the kind of fasting I want: free those who are wrongly imprisoned; lighten the burden of those who work for you; let the oppressed go free; and remove the chains that bind people. Share your food with the hungry, and give shelter to the homeless. Give clothes to those who need them, and do not hide from relatives who need your help." (Isaiah 58:6-7)

Paul Louis Metzger says that justice is "making individuals, communities, and the cosmos whole, by upholding both goodness and impartiality."[32] Jim Wallis tells us that justice "is about repairing broken relationships both with other people and to structures."[33] Tony Evans describes justice this way: "Whatever you want God to do for you personally, you must be willing for Him to do through you to others."[34]

Jesus himself has quite a bit to say about justice. The Gospel of Luke tells us He was appointed "to bring Good News to the poor...to proclaim that captives will be released, that the blind will see, that the oppressed will be set free." In the book of Matthew, we discover what is known as the Sermon on the Mount, Jesus' most well-known sermon in the Bible. Perhaps it is here where we gain the most insight into what is on Jesus' heart; it is where we learn about what is sometimes called the upside-down Kingdom. He tells us:

> "God blesses those who are poor and realize their need for him, for the Kingdom of Heaven is theirs. God blesses those who mourn, for they will be comforted. God blesses those who are humble, for they will inherit the whole earth. God blesses those who hunger and thirst for justice, for they will be satisfied. God blesses those who are merciful, for they will be shown mercy." (Matthew 5:3-7)

That is just the beginning. He goes on later in His sermon:

> "You have heard the law that says the punishment must match the injury: 'An eye for an eye, and a tooth for a tooth.' But I say, do not resist an evil person! If someone slaps you on the right cheek, offer the other also. If you are sued in court and your shirt is taken from you, give your coat, too. If a soldier demands that you carry his gear for a mile, carry it two miles. Give to those who ask, and don't turn away from those who want to borrow. You have heard the law that says, 'Love your neighbor' and hate your enemy. But I say, love your enemies! Pray for those who persecute you. In that way, you will be acting as true children of your Father in heaven. For he gives his sunlight to both the evil and the good, and he sends rain on the just and unjust alike. If you only love those who love you, what reward is there for that?" (Matthew 5:38-46)

We have a responsibility then, as Christians, to love both our neighbors and those we see as enemies. But, to love them both requires knowing them both.

The Role of Forgiveness in Justice

Quite possibly the most challenging and counterintuitive component of justice is forgiveness. If you are a follower of Christ, you are called to continuous forgiveness when it comes to the injustices done against us. I must forgive my bullies, not so that I can move from anger to apathy, but so that I treat them with a love that is as though I was never wronged.

This sort of forgiveness may seem absurd if you've never encountered the grace of God before. To most people, the idea of forgiving their abuser or their loved one's murderer seems inconceivable. Yet, that is exactly what Jesus has done for each one of us when it came to administering justice.

Corrie ten Boom's story is well known, demonstrating the power of forgiveness in the face of injustice. Her story began when she and her family were captured by the Nazis during World War II after hiding Jews in their home. Corrie and her sister Betsie were kept in a concentration camp, Betsie dying later the same year. Following her release from the camp, Corrie began a ministry to help rehabilitate concentration camp survivors, later expanding her work to 60 countries.

In a 1972 *Guideposts* article, Corrie recalls an encounter in 1947 with one of the former concentration camp guards at a church in Munich:

> "And that's when I saw him, working his way forward against the others. One moment I saw the overcoat and the brown hat; the next, a blue

uniform and a visored cap with its skull and crossbones.

"It came back with a rush: the huge room with its harsh overhead lights, the pathetic pile of dresses and shoes in the center of the floor, the shame of walking naked past this man. I could see my sister's frail form ahead of me, ribs sharp beneath the parchment skin. Betsie, how thin you were!

"Now he was in front of me, hand thrust out: 'A fine message, fräulein! How good it is to know that, as you say, all our sins are at the bottom of the sea!'

"And I, who had spoken so glibly of forgiveness, fumbled in my pocketbook rather than take that hand. He would not remember me, of course–how could he remember one prisoner among those thousands of women?

"But I remembered him and the leather crop swinging from his belt. It was the first time since my release that I had been face to face with one of my captors and my blood seemed to freeze.

"'You mentioned Ravensbrück in your talk,' he was saying. 'I was a guard in there.' No, he did not remember me.

"'But since that time,' he went on, 'I have become a Christian. I know that God has forgiven me for the cruel things I did there, but I would like to hear it from your lips as well. Fräulein'–again the hand came out–'will you forgive me?'

"And I stood there—I whose sins had every day to be forgiven—and could not. Betsie had died in that place—could he erase her slow terrible death simply for the asking?

"Those who were able to forgive their former enemies were able also to return to the outside world and rebuild their lives, no matter what the physical scars. Those who nursed their bitterness remained invalids. It was as simple and as horrible as that.

"And still I stood there with the coldness clutching my heart. But forgiveness is not an emotion—I knew that too. Forgiveness is an act of the will, and the will can function regardless of the temperature of the heart.

"'Jesus, help me!' I prayed silently. 'I can lift my hand. I can do that much. You supply the feeling.'

"And so woodenly, mechanically, I thrust my hand into the one stretched out to me. And as I did, an incredible thing took place. The current started in my shoulder, raced down my arm, sprang into our joined hands. And then this healing warmth seemed to flood my whole being, bringing tears to my eyes.

"'I forgive you, brother!' I cried. 'With all my heart!'

"For a long moment we grasped each other's hands, the former guard and the former prisoner. I had never known God's love so intensely as I did then."[35]

When I read this story about Corrie ten Boom, it occured to me that she needed to find compassion for the former guard in order to also find forgiveness for him. In this way, then, I would offer that a *requirement* of justice is that we have both compassion and forgiveness toward others. It means being willing to suffer alongside our brothers and sisters to see that their needs are met. It means forgiving our enemies and loved ones alike for the injustices they enacted upon us.

Bearing One Another's Burdens

This forgiving, compassionate kind of justice can be a challenge to Christians for a host of reasons, the first of which reveals a clash with the Western ideal of independence and self-determination. We have been conditioned to believe that being self-sufficient is a signal that we've achieved success, a signal that permeates how we have built our communities for decades. But how do we do justice, as the bible says to, when self-sufficiency is achieved? After all, does not the very idea of self-sufficiency go against the heart of God? In *Generous Justice*, Timothy Keller asks, "If we are never obliged to relieve others' burdens but only when we can do it without burdening ourselves, then how do we bear our neighbor's burdens, when we bear no burden at all?"[36]

What Keller is saying here is that if we are actually doing justice, it will be uncomfortable. That, perhaps, we need to be willing to put aside our conveniences to give someone else an opportunity to find freedom. Maybe it is part of our role to see that there is greater equity in how our resources are shared.

"There is an inequitable distribution of both goods and opportunities in this world," Keller says. "Therefore, if you have been assigned the goods of this world by God and you don't share them with others, it isn't just stinginess, it is injustice."

This will mean more than simply clearing out our closets, dropping an extra twenty dollar bill in the offering plate, or giving up a Saturday morning or two to volunteer at the local food bank. Those are all good things to do, of course, and we must continue to do them. But, these acts alone don't address the deeper needs that seem to ensnare our neighbors. They don't house the half-million million men, women, and children who live out on the streets here in the United States[37]. They don't assist the 11 million households who must pay more than half their income to have shelter[38]. And, they don't offer a safe place for the 70 million refugees forced from their homes across the globe due to violence and persecution[39].

These numbers are difficult to comprehend. But, we must remind ourselves that these don't represent numbers at all, but rather people with families, with feelings, with hearts ready to be met with love and joy from another being.

A Path to Justice

Another challenge Christians face when it comes to doing justice occurs when we see others as targets of evangelism, rather than foremost as humans fearfully and wonderfully made by God. The fate of our eternity is vital, as Romans 3 tells us that "we all fall short of God's glorious standard." But, while sharing the gospel is a means to justice, it is by no means the enactment of justice in itself.

"It's a compelling argument," says Robert D. Lupton, to believe that sharing the gospel is the most loving act we can do toward others. But that line of thinking falls short of enacting justice. As Lupton wrote in *Compassion, Justice and the Christian Life*, an evangelism-first approach,

> "leads toward viewing others as souls instead of people. And when we opt for rescuing souls over loving neighbors, compassionate acts can soon degenerate into evangelism techniques; pressing human needs depreciate in importance, and the spirit becomes the only thing worth caring about… When we skip over the Great Commandment on the way to fulfilling the Great Commission, we do great harm to the authenticity of faith."[40]

In the midst of bullying, discrimination, inequality, slavery, addiction, and violence, the very idea of achieving justice seems distant. Even so, the pursuit of justice for humanity is only the beginning of our commitment as followers of Jesus. "Justice is minimalist," says John Piper. "We don't get justice in the gospel; we get grace…Christ will be known in the culture when we treat people better than they deserve, not as they deserve."[41]

So, then, how do we get there? How do we achieve justice? Feeding and clothing people in need is just the start of enacting justice. It also means responding to *why* those in need are naked or hungry. While it's tempting to blame others for their misfortunes, to emphasize poor personal choices for their lot in life, this approach completely discounts the series of systemic privileges afforded to some and not others that have contributed to the depth of their success or failure.

Our cities, therefore, must be places where diversity is not just tolerated, but celebrated. Cities will be where assimilation is a product of cultures being immersed in one another, not a result of requiring that outsiders conform to what Ken Wytsma calls in his book *The Myth of Equality* the "white normative standard," or the practice of measuring cultural appropriateness based on white Anglo norms.[42] The privileges enjoyed by the majority culture since the 18th Century must be dissolved, at least in part, until *all* can not only experience the freedoms embodied in Western ideals, but more so the beauty that lies in the grace of God.

Cities will be places where Christians and their churches have not escaped to leave behind those whose immobility has destined them to a mirrored maze of need. Instead, the people of God will be firmly rooted in neighborhoods where they will know their neighbors, see each person for who they are—diverse not just in skin tone or income, but also in potential. Cities will be places where all can afford to thrive, both in the physical sense and the spiritual sense. Housing, transportation, education, employment, and health won't be afforded to some at the expense of others. Reconciliation and relationship will be present, not just between us but between us and our environment as well.

CHAPTER 7
LIFE WITH MORE

Based on 2018 estimates, roughly 12 percent of Americans live below the poverty line[1]. That equates to about 38 million people surviving on incomes below that of a full-time minimum wage worker. But, by and large, Americans are comparatively wealthy. We are the eighth-richest nation, per capita—above other developed nations like the Netherlands and Australia, but below others like Norway, Qatar, and Switzerland[2].

America is home to the wealthiest men and women alive. The world's richest men, Amazon's Jeff Bezos and Microsoft co-founder Bill Gates, each have a net worth in excess of $100 billion, with Warren Buffett close behind[3]. In fact, 14 of the top 20 richest people in the world live in the United States. There are also more millionaires in the U.S. than ever before—nearly 12 million people can say they have a seven-figure net worth[4].

We enjoy a host of comforts not experienced in many other places. Americans spend more each year in hair and nail salons than the entire GDP of countries like Belarus and Croatia[5, 6]. We also spend about $75 billion a year on our pets[7], and a staggering $860 billion eating out[8]. More than 60 million of us have paid subscriptions to a music streaming service[9], and the majority of households stream our TV and movie content through platforms like Netflix and Hulu[10]. Roughly 61 million Americans, or one out of every five people, have a gym membership[11].

Another area we spend a lot of money on is clothing. Americans spent $341 billion on clothing in 2018, much of it in the world that is known as "fast fashion."[12] We've gone from having four seasons of fashion to an almost weekly cycle of fast fashion. Aside from the implications that this level of mass production and consumption has on our planet, it also encourages impulse buying at a level not experienced by previous generations: if you might want this item in your closet, you have to buy it now, for it won't be here next week, much less next month.

And when it comes to our cars, we continue to buy bigger and bigger. Americans now spend an average of $38,000 for their four wheels, increasingly preferring larger SUVs and trucks over cars[13]. The top three best-selling vehicles in America are pickup trucks and more than half of the top 20 best-sellers are either trucks or SUVs[14]. But, because our salaries aren't keeping pace with the price of the cars we want, we are financing those pricier vehicles over longer terms, taking six years on average to pay them off[15].

If there's any area of our lives where our nature of consumption is expressed most, it's in the American home. The National Association of Home Builders reported that 6 million homes were bought and sold in 2019[16]. If you include both buyers and renters, about one in ten families move each year[17], which is a boon to retailers that sell household goods, moving supplies, furniture, and hardware. Our transient nature is also big business for services like moving companies, truck rental companies, and self storage facilities. According to SpareFoot, the self storage industry is worth $38 billion a year, with nearly one in 10 households currently renting a storage unit[18]. Self storage is such big business, in fact, that one company is developing a luxury storage facility near Austin, Texas, that boasts amenities like an "owner's lounge" with a "panoramic view of Lake Travis and the Texas Hill Country."[19]

I find it fascinating that so many households decide they need storage units to hold their belongings, considering that the average American home has ballooned in size over the past half-century. With new homes averaging two-and-a-half times larger than homes built in the 1950s, it starts to become apparent just how much more stuff we have accumulated.

In his book *House Lust*, Daniel McGinn coined the term *maximum use imperative*, defined as the tendency to consume with the most extreme use examples in mind[20]. It means believing we need a dining room that seats 12 people, even if the only meals eaten in the dining room happen on a few major holidays. It means having a large, comfortable guest room with ensuite bathroom, despite having overnight guests only a handful of nights a year. It means having an eight-seat SUV for a family of four, for the rare times extra children are in tow. And on and on it goes.

What exactly are we gaining when we buy the bigger house? Aside from the increased costs of heating and cooling the place, and the perceived need to furnish it all, we believe that room to store our things in large spaces might actually save us money. But does it really? Let's consider for a moment the bulk package of paper towels that many families buy at big box or warehouse stores. A 12-pack of premium paper towels currently costs about $16 at my local big box store. Those 12 rolls take up about 4 square feet of floor space which, given today's construction costs, means we spend about $600 just to build that space[21]. Amortized into a typical mortgage, that floor space devoted to the jumbo package of paper towels costs us more than $3.25 each month, quickly eating up any savings we think we're getting by buying in bulk. Naturally, we aren't just storing the extra paper towels. We have to have a place for the extra bottles of laundry detergent, the guest towels, the ice cream maker, the fine china, the old toys, and the obsolete electronics.

Now, if you're one of the few readers who actually uses all the rooms in your home, then I applaud you. It turns out that you are in the minority. Researchers from UCLA found that the families they studied used only about 40 percent of their home's square footage[22]. Most of the families' activity centered on the kitchen and family room, while formal living spaces and porches were rarely used.

Designer and writer Graham Hill had gotten fed up with moving around all his belongings from apartment to apartment, when he decided to rethink his relationship with stuff. In 2009, Hill bought two New York City apartments as an experiment to show people that we can design modern lifestyles into much smaller footprints[23]. The first LifeEdited project was a 420-square-foot apartment completely renovated to maximize the function in what most would consider a very tight space. It has movable walls, convertible furniture, and is curated with objects that slide, stack, and fold to make it much more usable than its hotel-room-size floor area would suggest. In fact, the apartment sleeps up to four people and can even comfortably seat 10 for a dinner party. Amazingly, Hill set out to take his experiment further, redesigning the second LifeEdited apartment with similar functionality (including the 10-person dinner party), but in just 350 square feet. While the cost to craft these smaller spaces might not differ much from building larger ones, the money saved in heating, cooling, and maintaining more efficient homes is substantial.

When I worked in the kitchen and bath industry, I got

sucked into all the product hype, believing that the new products we were selling would solve our clients' problems and, eventually, my own. I once attended the Kitchen and Bath Industry Show in Chicago, where literally tens of thousands of new products filled McCormick Place—the largest convention center in North America—to demonstrate how we could make the world a better place through cabinetry, appliances, fixtures, and accessories. I stared wide-eyed at new cooktops that would boil water in seconds instead of minutes, countertops made of lava rock, shower heads that doubled as speakers, and cabinets that would reveal and conceal a television with the touch of a button. This was all before the first iPhone came on the scene.

We all have been slowly and meticulously programmed to desire more. We won't feel content unless we have more apps available for our phones, more restaurants to try out, more charter schools for our children, more clothes in our closets, more followers on social media, more books on our shelves, more tools in our sheds. Advertisers spend a half-trillion dollars each year playing to our weaknesses, inundating our lives with print, audio, and video, campaigning to sell us everything from soda to software to sponges[24]. Women who subscribe to fashion magazines may not even recognize just how many of their pages are devoted to advertising rather than actual content. One analysis found that *Marie Claire* includes more than 225 ads within its pages, *Elle* fits in nearly 450 ads, and *Vogue* manages to cram more than 600 ads inside a single issue[25]. Product placement in movies and television dates back to the mid-20th Century, but has seemingly become more pronounced in recent years.

Likewise, we've also been convinced that the next thing will truly satisfy our desires. When that next smartphone comes out, then I'll be content. When I reach one thousand followers on

Twitter, then I'll be content. When I lose those last five pounds, then I'll be content. When I finally build that dream home with the big backyard and the kitchen with the double oven, then I'll be content. When I'm the boss, then I'll be content.

But, as researcher David G. Myers wrote two decades ago, "Thanks to our capacity to adapt to ever greater fame and fortune, yesterday's luxuries can soon become today's necessities and tomorrow's relics."[26] Apps and restaurants and books and Twitter followers are all fine. Many of us could stand to lose five pounds, or a little more in my case. Maybe you're about to have a child and that one-bedroom apartment isn't gonna cut it anymore. All of that is good. But when you and I decide that these are the tipping points to satisfaction or happiness, we have missed out on something much bigger. We have missed out on the truth.

When Jesus told the rich young man to sell his belongings and give them to the poor, it wasn't because Jesus said that having possessions was bad. Jesus doesn't tell us that the way to heaven is to give away all our stuff. When I read this account in the gospels of Matthew and Mark, the man is basically asking Jesus, "What else do I need to do?" In these man's words I hear, "I've tried everything. I've got the cash to buy whatever I want. I've tried to fill the spaces with things, with whatever I could get my hands on in order to have the perfect life. I have everything I could want and, yet, something is missing."

It's easy when we discuss wealth to focus on our stuff, but it's worth pointing out that wealth isn't just about our possessions. Often, our drive for more also pushes us to seek position and popularity, and to celebrate those who have attained those things. We are not content to be co-laborers, we want to be the CEO. We don't just want to hear a thanks for a job well-done, we want others to know how great of a job we did. We don't just want to be on the winning team, we want to be the M.V.P.

If there was ever an M.V.P. in Christian history, it was the apostle Paul. No stranger to the power of position, Paul wrote to the church in Philippi, an early church plant in what is now northeastern Greece, explaining that he once had everything going for him:

> "...I could have confidence in my own effort if anyone could. Indeed, if others have reason for confidence in their own efforts, I have even more! ...I am a pure-blooded citizen of Israel and a member of the tribe of Benjamin—a real Hebrew if there ever was one! I was a member of the Pharisees, who demand the strictest obedience to the Jewish law. I was so zealous that I harshly persecuted the church. And as for righteousness, I obeyed the law without fault." (Philippians 3:4-6)

But here's where Paul pivoted:

> "I once thought these things were valuable, but now I consider them worthless because of what Christ has done." (v. 7)

Did you catch that? Paul did not just say that being an Israeli citizen is less valuable than being a follower of Christ. His mantra was not "God first, Israel second." He declared it *worthless*. He went on a bit later in his letter:

> "...I have learned how to be content with whatever I have. I know how to live on almost nothing or with everything. I have learned the secret of living in every situation, whether it is with a full stomach or empty, with plenty or little." (Philippians 4:11-12)

Simplicity

In his book *Inside-Out Simplicity*, Joshua Becker writes, "simplicity is freedom from the passion to possess." He acknowledges that possessions themselves are not inherently bad, but that when we are compelled to have them, they consequently have us. Richard J. Foster held nothing back in his 1981 book, *Freedom of Simplicity*, calling our lust for things "psychotic." He reminded us that Christian simplicity "brings sanity to our compulsive extravagance, and peace to our frantic spirit." This simplicity "lives in harmony with the ordered complexity of life."

What does it mean for Christians to live simply? After all, it's not as though I'm calling on any of you out there to move to a monastery, living only with a bed, a bible, a lamp, and a few pieces of clothing. Maybe for you it means simply rethinking your relationship with your stuff—spending time reflecting on whether you have possessions or they have you. It might mean reclaiming time back from your lifestyle, purging the junk that actually costs you time, money, and mental energy to hold onto. That could mean getting rid of those fussy clothes that require the hefty dry cleaning bill. That could mean dumping that boat you've spent thousands maintaining for just a few hours of summer fun. That could mean bidding adieu to the treadmill, the old toddler bed, or even that boombox that's been collecting dust since the 90s.

For others of you, simplifying your life might mean simplifying your location. This will surely sound strange to some of you, but simplicity may not actually be found in the suburbs, as decades of advertising has promised, but rather in more urban locales. Homebuilders use descriptors like "peace and quiet," "relaxed," and "serene" to describe the subdivisions they build today, but the reality of these neighborhoods can sometimes be anything but. Residents of off-the-beaten-path places are often subjected to arduous commutes that elevate our stress hormones, are separated from their daily needs by major roads, and tend to be isolated from their neighbors. Homeowners' associations are often quick to pounce when one's grass is a little too tall or one's garbage cans are a little too visible. Criminal and drug activity, once associated primarily with inner cities, have migrated to the suburbs as well.

By contrast, urban living can actually offer back an important commodity in many of our lives: time. Choosing to live near your work and near the other things you need can save a tremendous amount of time, especially for the three percent of whom are called "super commuters," those workers who spend at least 90 minutes traveling to work[27]. The time we regain by choosing proximity over price-per-square-foot can add significant value to our family relationships, our friendships, our health, and our sanity. We are less likely to miss out on our kids' activities, less likely to get divorced, less likely to be obese, and less likely to die from preventable diseases or car crashes when we elect to live more compactly[28]. Charles Montgomery writes of the importance of proximity to family, friends, and even strangers, in *Happy City*:

> "As much as we complain about other people, there is nothing worse for mental health than a social desert...Social isolation just may be the greatest environmental hazard of city living— worse than noise, pollution, or even crowding. The more connected we are with family and community, the less likely we are to experience colds, heart attacks, strokes, cancer, and depression. Simple friendships with other people in

one's neighborhood are some of the best salves for stress during hard economic times—in fact, sociologists have found that when adults keep these friendships, their kids are better insulated from the effects of their parents' stress. Connected people sleep better at night. They are more able to tackle adversity. They live longer. They consistently report being happier."

Of course, to rent or buy a home in compact, urban neighborhoods—especially as a family with children—can cost more than it does in the suburbs. In a number of cities, housing expenses in core neighborhoods require an amount of wealth that not many of its residents have. So how, then, can families actively choose a neighborhood that offers more connectivity to other people?

For starters, we must reconsider our need for space. Do we really need two living spaces and two dining areas? Does every child *truly* need their own bedroom? Is a separate office really necessary? Do we need to be able to walk into every closet? And what use is that double-height foyer, really? What I've learned over the past 20 years of studying and practicing residential design is that more square footage does not always equate to more usable space.

Children in Cities

I recently had the opportunity to walk through several models of a new condominium development taking place near Vancouver, British Columbia. While most cities cater their housing toward young singles and childless couples, Vancouver has determined that its urban housing must also consider the needs of families with kids. Brent Toderian, consultant and former Chief Planner for Vancouver, says that children are an "indicator species of a healthy downtown."[29] As a result, developers there are required to design at least 25 percent of its housing units with two bedrooms and a minimum of 10 percent of the units with three bedrooms[30]. One of the models in this tower I visited managed to fit three bedrooms and two bathrooms into roughly 950 square feet, a level of efficiency virtually unheard of in today's housing landscape. Yet, the unit featured bedrooms large enough to accommodate at least full-size beds, bathrooms with tubs, a laundry closet, a kitchen with an island, and even a nook specially designed for a workspace. I've walked through many homes with twice the square footage that are not as thoughtfully planned as the units I saw in Vancouver. Moreover, families who live at this property will enjoy neighborhood amenities that can't be found in most traditional subdivisions, like a full-service grocery store, cafes, multiple parks, a public market, and walkable access to two train lines. Perhaps unsurprisingly, every unit in that tower (and two others) sold before construction even began.

Every city I've studied that has worked to accommodate children in its downtown has achieved exactly that result. Parents arrive with kids in tow, ready to enjoy the parks, museums, libraries, and other public spaces these downtowns have to offer. Chicago saw this phenomenon happen when it opened Millennium Park in 2004. Houston witnessed it with the opening of Discovery Green in 2008. Here in San Antonio, the ongoing reinvention of Hemisfair—the site of the 1968 World's Fair—is attracting families in numbers not seen in 50 years. Minneapolis reopened its downtown elementary school due to the growth of young families in its core. Nearly 5,000 children live in downtown Seattle now, prompting the local school district to plan for new schools to be built[31]. One *Seattle Times* article noted that the increase in school-aged children downtown is outpacing the growth in the rest of the Seattle school district[32].

Despite these shifts, I continue to hear well-meaning folks insist that cities are no place to raise children. They're unsafe, they're crowded, there are no places for kids to play, and it's too expensive. These statements have dominated our cultural norms for many decades, but I am inspired by the lives of families who have bucked that trend, having learned what it means to thrive with kids in a more urban context.

Chris and Melissa Bruntlett sold their family car in 2010, embarking on the journey of raising children in Vancouver car-lite. Living in a more compact setting, Melissa told me, offers her family the ability to know their neighbors better and share in their daily activities with them. And, replacing the typical freeway commute with walking and biking, Chris said, "means more time we can invest in our community and in our family." Their car-lite lifestyle inspired them to launch Modacity, a media platform that uses video, photography, and writing to document the joys of the casual and commuter bicycling lifestyle. Much of Modacity's content features kids pedaling right alongside mom and dad, as well as photos and video of people riding cargo bicycles to transport large items like furniture and Christmas trees. The success of Modacity has since brought the Bruntletts to The Netherlands, where they both now work for organizations that promote active transportation.

Adrian Crook, another Vancouver resident, has made a name for himself by documenting a life where he raises his five children in a downtown high-rise apartment. His blog, 5 Kids 1 Condo, helps aspiring urban families, teaching them how he tames the tornado of toys that could easily overwhelm his 1,000-square-foot space, not to mention how to maintain a sense of privacy among his herd. What Crook has found over the years is that his children need far less stuff than we are led to believe and, thus, he has embraced a minimalist lifestyle that gives breathing room both to his mind and his bank account. "Will kids tell you they want a big house and lots of stuff? Of course," Adrian told me. "But living closer together builds empathy and helps kids understand what they really need in order to thrive. It turns out that quality of life has little to do with standard of living."

Freed *for* More

It is important that we each ask ourselves this important question: what does our wealth free us for? I realize the wording of that question may seem a bit strange. After all, society tells us that money frees us in a host of ways, the biggest assertion being that having more will relieve our worry. But, what we read in the Bible is quite a bit different. In Revelation, Jesus tells the church in Smyrna (what is today Izmir, Turkey) that their suffering and poverty make them rich:

> "I know about your suffering and your poverty— but you are rich! I know the blasphemy of those opposing you...Don't be afraid of what you are about to suffer. The devil will throw some of you into prison to test you. You will suffer for ten days. But if you remain faithful even when facing death, I will give you the crown of life." (Revelation 2:9-10)

The Christians living in this city endured abject poverty with few material possessions and, to top it off, they were being persecuted by others who claimed to be Jewish—even to the point of death. Yet, their ability to stay true to God in the face of intense oppression offered them a reward that could never be bought.

In contrast, Jesus has a very different message to the nearby church in Laodicea:

> "I know all the things you do, that you are neither hot nor cold. I wish that you were one or the other! But since you are like lukewarm water, neither hot nor cold, I will spit you out of my mouth! You say, 'I am rich. I have everything I want. I don't need a thing!' And you don't realize that you are wretched and miserable and poor and blind and naked." (Revelation 3:15-17)

Wretched. Miserable. These are harsh words, no doubt, and certainly not words we would typically use to describe someone with a lot of zeros in their bank account. But, what I believe Jesus is ultimately communicating to us is that freedom is not found in self-sufficiency. One Bible commentator actually calls self-sufficiency "the death-knell of relationship with God."[33] The gospel of John uses an illustration of a vine and branches to remind us of our dependence on Him: "Yes, I am the vine; you are the branches. Those who remain in me, and I in them, will produce much fruit. For apart from me you can do nothing." (John 15:5)

In his book *More or Less*, Jeff Shinabarger says: "The more self-sufficient we are, the less we need others. The less we need others, the less likely we are to form the bonds of true community.

Convenience enhances self-reliance, increases ease, and ironically, separates us from real relationships with people who have real needs." So, what then?

The answer to our dangerous self-sufficiency is not to become poor, but to become generous. I will even go further and say that our wealth has no value, then, but when our hands are open, when we are at our most generous. When I ask, "what does our wealth free us for?" I am prompting us to think about what good we can do with the resources that have been entrusted to us.

I was struck by the stark contrast of a humanity that chooses generosity and one that chooses stinginess. As Hurricane Harvey blew through the Texas coast in August 2017, damaging thousands of homes and submerging hundreds of Houston-area neighborhoods under several feet of water, regular people across the country mobilized to aid strangers in need. Squads of people with flat-bottomed motorboats descended into the chaos, rescuing people around the clock who had been trapped in their homes and vehicles. Some showed up to find pets that had been left behind by families forced to abandon their homestead. Many others pooled together resources to try and put a dent in the need created by the massive storm.

Meanwhile, as the reality of Houston's condition set in, fear of a gasoline shortage quickly spread across Texas and other parts of the country, sending people into a buying frenzy that quickly depleted supplies. Rather than prompting us to conserve our energy, instead residents arrived at gas stations in vehicles filled with extra containers, hoarding all that was left and leaving many would-be Labor Day travelers without the necessary fuel for their holiday road trips. Within a matter of hours, thousands of gas stations were sucked dry and, as tankers arrived to replenish a station, lines of cars blocked traffic in hopes of filling up. San Antonio's mayor tried to reassure residents that a real supply problem did not exist, hoping to stave off the hoarding[34]. Instead, after five days with little sign of reprieve, the city's public transportation system announced it would allow people to ride its buses for free to help folks get around[35].

The Bible is clear about what our attitude should be toward wealth. In the book of 1 Timothy, Paul writes:

> "Teach those who are rich in this world not to be proud and not to trust in their money, which is so unreliable. Their trust should be in God, who richly gives us all we need for our enjoyment. Tell them to use their money to do good. They should be rich in good works and generous to those in need, always being ready to share with others. By doing this they will be storing up their treasure as a good foundation for the future so that they may experience true life." (1 Timothy 6:17-19)

Always be ready to share. This statement can produce a great amount of anxiety in us, particularly because there are already so many demands on our resources. The more we earn, the more it seems we need in order to prop up our lifestyle. The Bureau of Labor Statistics reports that the average household spends over $650 every month on food, around $800 per month on transportation, and more than $250 a month on entertainment[36]. On top of that, Americans owe an average $7,000 to credit card companies and have nearly $50,000 in student loan debt, leaving us little left to share with anyone[37]. In fact, one out of every five Americans actually spends more in a year than they earn, which means 20 percent of us literally have no margin in our budgets to share with others[38]. How, then, can we deliver on our call to generosity when we have leveraged everything entrusted to us for the comforts of this life?

Perhaps one reason our call to generosity can be so anxiety-producing is that our wealth has already made us anxious. As it turns out, research shows us that richer people—and richer nations, generally—demonstrate higher rates of anxiety and anxiety disorders than those with lower incomes[39]. While the science on anxiety disorders is far from settled, researchers found that as many as eight percent of Australians, New Zealanders, and Americans will experience clinical levels of anxiety during their lifetime. Citizens of poorer nations like Poland and Nigeria have less than a one percent chance of experiencing an anxiety disorder.

Once we have devoted our wealth to the things of the world, we cannot devote it to anything else. As the gospels of Matthew and Luke both tells us, "No one can serve two masters. For you will hate one and love the other; you will be devoted to one and despise the other. You cannot serve God and be enslaved to money." (Matthew 6:24; Luke 16:13)

It is for this reason that, throughout this book, I have been making the argument that the pursuit of community—and, particularly, the environments that foster it—helps us to effectively live Christ's mandate to love our neighbors. If we are focused on what we can gain from society, instead of on what we can contribute, we will not love our neighbors well. If we devote our resources only to elevating ourselves, we cannot be devoted to the needs of others.

Entering into a meaningful community goes beyond just a "thou shalt" kind of mandate, though. Community reminds us we have shared interests, shared goals, and often shared anxieties.

It reminds us that we matter. "You are important—not because you're rich, but because you are human," Charles Montgomery wrote in *Happy City*. But, the more we choose places, experiences, and things over the richness of community, the more we need those things to tell us we are important, and the more we lose the capacity to remind others that they, too, are beloved. Jeff Shinabarger writes: "The conveniences that we increasingly convince ourselves are necessary for a happy or successful life also separate us from those who do not have them. The more layers of convenience we add to our lives, the more space we create between us and those desperately working day to day to survive."[40]

In addressing the communal value that can come from living in an urban setting, there is a real risk in seeing city living as a status object in itself. Much in the same way we were programmed since the end of World War II to believe suburban life makes us superior to those "left behind" in cities, we can also find ourselves trapped in the modern-day belief that urbanism advances us over those living in sprawl. As wealth has facilitated flight from the perceived ills of living in city centers, wealth can also propagate the perceived exclusivity of being back in the core. As Christians, we must reject both extremes.

Generosity and our readiness to share are not solely dependent on our address, but our address matters nonetheless. If we are to find ourselves connected with those who have both more and less than we do, or at least ready to encounter the stranger mentioned so often in Scripture, we will need to take an honest look at how the lifestyles we've built either help or hinder us in that process. Could someone who earns a lower income than your own afford to live nearby? Are you likely to run into others from your neighborhood while on your daily routine? Could you even walk to an amenity where neighbors might go or use public transportation to get around town?

As a planner, I find plenty of promise in policies that tear down the walls otherwise resulting in neighborhoods of economic or racial sameness. For years, I have been intrigued by places like Chatham Square in Alexandria, Virginia, where apartments for lower-income families are seamlessly integrated with million-dollar townhomes; or Mueller, the desirable Austin, Texas, community where more than a quarter of its homes are reserved for families earning modest incomes. While neighborhoods like these require limited subsidies to make this kind of integration possible, a proposition I recognize is unpopular with some, there are other things communities are beginning to do to build diversity into neighborhoods. In Miami, exempting downtown housing from minimum parking requirements is believed to lower rents by as much as $330 per month, according to a *Forbes* article[41]. In California, a bill was passed in 2015 allowing developers that offer affordable homes to provide less parking if it is near public transportation[42]. Others still are looking at how regulations like minimum lot sizes, caps on density, and height limitations could be revisited to better encourage neighborhood diversity.

Wherever we ultimately choose to live, whether we continue to spread into the suburbs or if we continue the regrowth of our urban centers (realistically, both will continue), our focus must be on how our decisions strengthen our relationships with one another and ready us to the blessedness of generosity. Every dollar in and out are stewarded to us for God's purposes which, of course, are centered on loving Him and loving our neighbors. To the life that calls our attention away from these things—the tendency toward compulsive consumption and segregationist communities—we say, enough is enough.

CHAPTER 8
LIFE WITH LESS

Few people ever become poor on purpose. Being sworn in as an AmeriCorps VISTA volunteer, however, requires just that commitment. More than 8,000 people take that step each year, not just for the sake of experiencing poverty, but to combat it[1]. VISTAs are connected with nonprofit organizations across the United States, developing and engaging in programs designed to alleviate the injustices that nearly 40 million Americans experience in their daily lives.

When I enlisted as a VISTA for a one-year term in 2008, I bid farewell to two-thirds of my income (and my home state) to work with a Central Texas-based organization that helped link people with disabilities to an array of services. My role was to develop a database of housing options in the Waco region that could accommodate households where at least one of its members had a disability. For some, it meant finding a home that was wheelchair accessible which, among other things, included widened doorways and a roll-in shower. With many of the city's apartments built before the signing of the Americans with Disabilities Act in 1990, this was no simple task. Yet, as much as I was tasked with finding housing with the necessary physical features to accommodate people with disabilities, my job required finding housing that was affordable to them. "If you have a disability in the U.S., you're twice as likely to be poor as someone without a disability," said Pam Fessler on *National Public Radio* in 2015[2]. The majority of households we served survived on less than $1,000 per month. In fact, the average disability benefit paid monthly in 2019 was just $1,234, about $15,000 annually[3]. But, if a person's disability is severe enough that a work history is impossible, the benefits paid out by the federal government are even lower.

As a VISTA, I also qualified for one of the country's most politically controversial safety net programs, the Supplemental Nutrition Assistance Program, or SNAP. Also known as food stamps, I was provided a card (called the Lone Star Card in Texas) I could use to buy groceries, supplementing the small stipend I received as a full-time volunteer. There is a great deal of stigma associated with the use of SNAP in America, a reality I became aware of the first time I used my Lone Star Card.

Before becoming a VISTA I probably spent more time judging the spending habits of America's poor than I care to admit. It's easy to justify buying non-essentials when we have expendable income, but hard not to question a mother whose young children are all wearing brand-name shoes while she pays for groceries with food stamps. It's hard not to ask why she's buying the four dollar package of cheese, while you scrape by on the package of "cheese food product." It's hard not to judge when she piles the kids and the groceries into her shiny SUV, while you're driving a dull compact sedan.

In reality, I cannot begin to understand the circumstances of that mother and her children. It's not my place to question how she got the shoes and the SUV and the expensive cheese. In fact, holding my own Lone Star Card, using government food stamp money to make ends meet, I worried that there were others like me out there, turning their nose up at my supposed misuse of funds. Did they wonder why their tax dollars were helping pay for my food? I mean, I don't fit the face of poverty, right?

There's a good chance that, unlike me, that mother did not choose a life of poverty. What if she worked many hours of overtime to give her children those shoes? What if the SUV was something she purchased before her husband left her, when financial times were better?

Even as I attempted, all those years ago, to rectify the thoughts of my heart by giving this woman a good reason to be poor, I still do not fully understand poverty. I sometimes fail at separating stereotypes from reality. I fail at pursuing justice for the sake of that mother's children, so that they may have a way out of poverty one day.

Both before I became a VISTA and after I returned to the workforce, I have been surrounded by the pervasive belief that people in poverty can will themselves out of that state. Perhaps less obvious in that belief is the implication that people willed themselves into poverty in the first place. But, tied in with injustice is the understanding that systems often select those who will be poor. Those same systems determine the likelihood they will stay there.

Consider the life of an infant boy born into an impoverished family today. After being less likely to have received proper medical care and nutrition while in utero, that baby is more likely to experience significant stress that can lead to delayed brain development[4]. He is more likely to grow up in a home with lead-based paint[5], in a neighborhood with significantly worse air quality than wealthier neighborhoods[6]. These exposures increase the risk he will have developmental problems as well as breathing disorders like asthma[7], resulting in more frequent illnesses that lead to increased absences and lower performance in school.

As he grows, being poor will also mean he is less likely to eat a proper diet, often showing up to school hungry. Hunger, unsurprisingly, will mean he is less able to concentrate in his classes, less able to remember what he is taught, and more likely to perform poorly on exams[8]. With few resources at home, he is unlikely to study or do homework there. As he falls further behind, he is more prone to experiencing anxiety, depression, and other behavioral problems[9]. He's also more likely to repeat a grade[10].

On top of the issues he is likely to face in school, his home environment is also likely to be a challenge. Today, he is likely to live in a single-parent home, particularly if he is Latino or African American[11]. Despite stereotypes, his mother (the most likely present parent) *is* employed, but often in low-wage jobs with irregular hours that offer few, if any, benefits[12]. Like nearly three-quarters of families in poverty, his mother dedicates the majority of her income to housing, increasing the likelihood they will fall behind on rent and be forced to move at some point[13]. In *Evicted*, Matthew Desmond points out that some 16,000 adults and children are evicted each year in the city of Milwaukee, Wisconsin alone. At best, it means this young boy will be forced to transfer schools often, subjected to different curricula and teaching styles that put him further behind. At worst, he will become homeless at some point during his childhood.

Given his tenuous housing situation and worsening school performance, there is a high risk this boy will drop out of high school altogether. In fact, as Matthew Lynch, Ed.D. wrote, poor students are ten times more likely to drop out of high school than students from high-income families[14]. This is particularly true for children from homes where parents also did not complete high school. Being a dropout, then, would mean this young man will earn dramatically less than high school and college graduates, be employed in less stable jobs, and perpetuate the cycle of poverty.

There are a host of ways America's poor are disadvantaged that are largely outside of their individual control. The poor tend to pay more for a range of goods and services including groceries, insurance coverage, loans, and technology[15, 16]. Much of this stems from the isolation that many low-income families face in neighborhoods where the vast majority of their neighbors are also poor. It is a very real isolation, where even public transportation access fails to adequately connect America's poor to quality goods, stable employment, healthcare services, and decent schools. A Harvard University study found that longer commute times were associated with lower economic mobility[17]. In other words, poor families that are far from work are likelier to stay poor. A similar study showed communities with inadequate transportation access experience higher rates of unemployment than communities with better transit access[18].

Speaking of isolation, perhaps the most troubling evidence of poverty exists among our most disconnected demographic— the elderly. Many older adults are poor in America, mostly by design. "People are living longer, more expensive lives," wrote Mary Jordan and Kevin Sullivan in *The Washington Post*. "Record numbers of Americans older than 65 are working — now nearly 1 in 5. That proportion has risen steadily over the past decade, and at a far faster rate than any other age group."

Jordan and Sullivan continued:

> "While some work by choice rather than need, millions of others are entering their golden years with alarmingly fragile finances. Fundamental

changes in the U.S. retirement system have shifted responsibility for saving from the employer to the worker, exacerbating the nation's rich-poor divide. Two recent recessions devastated personal savings. And at a time when 10,000 baby boomers are turning 65 every day, Social Security benefits have lost about a third of their purchasing power since 2000.

"Polls show that most older people are more worried about running out of money than dying."[19]

Safety Net or Hammock?

Another challenge facing America's poor is what's been popularly referred to as the "welfare cliff." The idea is that there are distinct income cut-offs for varying poverty alleviation programs, suggesting that if a worker were to receive a raise that pushes them outside eligible status for the program, their real income would actually fall. A 2014 analysis revealed that a single parent household with two children in the Chicago area actually benefits most through welfare programs if the parent earns an hourly wage of about $12 per hour[20]. To "recover" the loss in the value of the combined assistance programs, the parent would need to earn about $38 per hour. And, if that same parent earned $18 per hour, the value of that employment would actually be less than if he or she did not work at all but was able to, instead, receive the full array of welfare benefits available to the family.

Journalists have done quite a bit to point out the flaws in that study, including the fact that few, if any, families would actually see the dollar value of benefits they receive. More critically, few families actually receive all the benefits they are eligible for. One analysis revealed that, in most states, fewer than one in five recipients of cash welfare benefits actually receive housing subsidies for which they are eligible, because there aren't enough of the subsidy dollars to go around[21]. The National Low Income Housing Coalition reported that wait lists for subsidized housing across the country are the norm, with a quarter of large cities reporting wait lists more than 7 years long[22]. Nonetheless, all of this points to a system that actually provides few opportunities to overcome the many barriers that exist for exiting poverty.

Unfortunately, the flaws built into assistance programs have led some of our politicians to conclude that subsidizing the needs of America's poor is ineffectual and fosters dependency on government benefits. Economic research has largely debunked these persistent myths, including one international study, showing no evidence that welfare programs discourage employment[23]. It is not that poverty alleviation programs have transformed from a "safety net" into a "hammock," as Paul Ryan famously suggested back in 2012[24]; rather, it is that the poor are most vulnerable to job loss due to recessions and family or health emergencies. Regarding the suggestion that assistance programs discourage the poor from seeking employment, John Aziz writes:

> "I don't dispute that cutting welfare would make job-seekers more desperate. But that is not the same thing as creating more jobs. Without a strong enough supply of jobs for current levels of job seekers, pushing more people into the job market is a recipe for desperation and misery rather than economic growth. It might lead to more trinket-sellers and window-washers at the roadside (as well as more thieves, hustlers,

prostitutes, and beggars), but there is no guarantee that any of these people would make enough
money to support themselves or their families."[25]

Aziz goes on to say, "It is foolish to enact measures that
make the jobless more desperate for a job," and that the first
meaningful step to helping people in poverty find jobs is to create
them.

When it comes to work, a significant challenge for those
in poverty is access to paid leave. Whereas the overwhelming
majority of high wage earners have access to paid sick days, less
than one-third of low-wage earners have that same access[26].
This means that families who already struggle to pay even their
basic living expenses are most penalized for staying home when
they or their children have a cold. These employees literally
cannot afford to be sick. In fact, there is no legal protection in
most places from being terminated from a job for taking a sick
day—even with a doctor's note. As one writer put it, "If your
employer is threatening to fire you if you miss work, then show
up on a stretcher if you have to."[27]

Industries of Poverty

Often ignored are the many ways in which our economy
has become dependent on low-wage workers and strives to keep
those workers earning too little to make ends meet. Oxfam, an
organization focused on ending poverty, found that nearly 42
million American workers earn less than $12 per hour[28]—an
hourly wage too low to rent a two-bedroom home anywhere
in the U.S.[29] About 1.5 million workers actually make less than
the federal minimum wage. We have seen dozens of industries
emerge and expand in recent decades, largely on the backs of

both low-wage American workers and even-lower-wage international workers.

Take coffee, for instance. In 1990, there were only about 1,600 coffee shops in America[30]. In 2019, there were more than 37,000 of them[31], fueling what is today an $80 billion industry in the U.S. alone[32]. But what does that coffee cost us, really? The typical barista earns around $11 per hour, including tips, which equates to a full-time annual salary of just over $23,000 (based on these numbers, a single barista can only afford to pay about $580 in housing expenses each month)[33]. More tragically, industry workers in places like Nicaragua and Kenya withstand harsh conditions for wages as little as a few dollars a day. Even here, the U.S. Department of Labor found in 2012 that some coffee plantations in Hawaii were violating a host of labor laws, paying workers less than minimum wage and even hiring young children to harvest coffee[34].

Another industry of both rapid growth and vast inequities is technology. With the first iPhone unveiled in 2007, followed by the Android in 2008, now more than 1.5 billion smartphones are produced and sold each year worldwide[35]. While the average salary for Apple's software engineers is well in excess of $100,000 per year[36], those who actually produce the phones in Chinese factories are paid less than a tenth of that, and that's accounting for the many hours of overtime required to meet the immense demand for the new devices released each year[37].

One last industry I'll mention here is the rapid expansion of retail goods that were barely on our radars a couple decades ago. Except for the shiny spandex bodysuits of 1980s aerobics videos, clothing specially made for exercise is a largely modern concept. These clothing lines came onto the scene beginning in the late 90s, replacing sweatpants and basic T-shirts as the predominant gym uniform with athletic apparel that has exploded into a $90 billion submarket here in North America alone.[38] As with nearly all other fast fashion, these clothes are sold in retail outlets by employees making relatively low wages, and are produced in consolidated factories by workers in South and Southeast Asia, earning as little as $68 *per month*[39].

—

In case I have been misunderstood up to this point, I am not suggesting that poverty is entirely out of people's control. People climb out of poverty every day, an accomplishment that should surely be celebrated. The Census Bureau reported that nearly 9 million people have climbed out of poverty in the United States since 2014[40, 41]. According to the World Bank, more than 1 billion people worldwide managed to escape extreme poverty between 1990 and 2013[42].

It is this last set of statistics that makes me think it is important to pause and define what poverty actually is. It's not just about whether someone is "broke." Generally, researchers and experts on the subject consider two measures of poverty: *absolute poverty*, which is the inability for a person or family to meet their basic food and shelter needs; and, *relative poverty*, which refers to the economic standing of an individual or family as compared to others in their society. While the specifics of both measures are criticized often due to their focus on income and consumption, they provide a decent starting point for understanding the gap between the haves and have-nots, as well as the ability of people to afford the basic cost of living. While absolute poverty, or extreme poverty, is understood to include earnings of less than US$1.90 per day, relative poverty is typically a percentage of the median income for a given area or region[43]. With the latter, then, a single person earning $12,000 in America would be considered impoverished, whereas that same income in Estonia would be more aligned with the nation's typical household earnings[44].

A danger for us is understanding this relativism between global poverty and Western poverty and believing that the poverty American families experience is not real. In other words, we are prone to downplay the needs of families living below the poverty line here when we recognize there are citizens of our planet earning far lower wages than what's offered in the U.S. While this may be true, strictly speaking, it fails to address the fact that staying housed or fed in America comes at a higher cost. This line of thinking also reveals in us our tendency to stratify people based on arbitrary measures and, thus, determine who is worthy of our help and who is not.

Regard for the Poor

It is revealing of our nature that we judge who is needy and who isn't, especially when the Bible does not point this out as our role. Throughout the Psalms, we read about God's heart to defend and rescue the poor, the needy, the widow, and the fatherless: "The Lord is a refuge for the oppressed, a stronghold in times of trouble" (Psalm 9:9); "You evildoers frustrate the plans of the poor, but the Lord is their refuge" (Psalm 14:6); "The wicked draw the sword and bend the bow to bring down the poor and needy, to slay those whose ways are upright" (Psalm 37:14); and "Defend the cause of the weak and fatherless; maintain the rights of the poor and oppressed. Rescue the weak and needy; deliver them from the hand of the wicked." (Psalm 82:3-4).

The same regard for the poor can be seen throughout Proverbs: "He who despises his neighbor sins, but blessed is he who is kind to the needy" (Proverbs 14:21); "He who mocks the poor shows contempt for their maker; whoever gloats over disaster will not go unpunished" (Proverbs 17:5); "He who oppresses the poor to increase his wealth and he who gives gifts to the rich—both come to poverty" (Proverbs 22:16); "The righteous care about justice for the poor, but the wicked have no such concern." (Proverbs 29:7)

During Jesus' ministry, we see a powerful moment where he declares his heart toward those in need. In Luke 4:14-30, he has just returned to his childhood home, a place where excitement had begun to build for what he was doing:

> "Then Jesus returned to Galilee, filled with the Holy Spirit's power. Reports about him spread quickly through the whole region. He taught regularly in their synagogues and was praised by everyone.

> "When he came to the village of Nazareth, his boyhood home, he went as usual to the synagogue on the Sabbath and stood up to read the Scriptures. The scroll of Isaiah the prophet was handed to him. He unrolled the scroll and found the place where this was written:

> "'The Spirit of the Lord is upon me,

> For he has anointed me to bring Good News to the poor.

> He has sent me to proclaim that captives will be released,

> That the blind will see,

That the oppressed will be set free,

And that the time of the Lord's favor has come.'

"He rolled up the scroll, handed it back to the attendant, and sat down. All eyes in the synagogue looked at him intently. Then he began to speak to them. 'The Scripture you've just heard has been fulfilled this very day!'" (Luke 4:14-21)

Of all the Old Testament passages he could have read to his neighbors, Jesus chose to share this excerpt from Isaiah 61. I suspect this was no accident. After all, His listeners have been anticipating a messiah that would bring vengeance on Israel's enemies as a means to justice, but that is not what Jesus says here. He doesn't just announce that he is the long-awaited messiah, but that his arrival has special significance for the vulnerable. It is truly a message of grace to the weak, one we learn later is met with rage:

"When they heard this, the people in the synagogue were furious. Jumping up, they mobbed him and forced him to the edge of the hill on which the town was built. They intended to push him over the cliff, but he passed right through the crowd and went on his way." (Luke 4:28-30)

Interestingly, Jesus' countercultural concern for the poor remains countercultural to this day. Our society celebrates those who have amassed any amount of wealth and gives little voice to those who live with less. Legislators often debate the merits of safety net programs, while largely ignoring those line items that benefit the middle and upper echelons of society. For example, the mortgage interest tax deduction is a nearly $40 billion-a-year subsidy that disproportionately benefits the rich[45]. Low-income homeowners and the nearly 37 percent of households that rent see virtually no benefit from this subsidy.

A refrain I sometimes hear from fellow Christians regarding America's safety net programs is that it is the Church's responsibility to provide these services to the poor. Surely, a number of churches operate their own social service ministries, while many others support the work of great relief organizations. Yet, if we believe it is truly the Church's role to aid humanity's needs, then we have some work to do. While researchers estimate that about 52 million Americans attend church regularly[46], only a fraction of those actually tithe. Protestant churches in the U.S. receive an average $17 per adult per week in the offering plate, which is hardly enough to keep the lights on for most church buildings, let alone feed, clothe, and house the needy[47]. If churchgoers actually tithed—that is, if we actually gave 10 percent of our income to churches—an additional $165 billion would be available every year for ministry and relief work, says Mike Holmes in *Relevant*[48]. For context, that additional amount is more than twice the federal budget for SNAP[49], seven times the budget for the Housing Choice (Section 8) Voucher program[50], and ten times the amount spent on Temporary Assistance for Needy Families (TANF)—more popularly referred to as welfare[51].

How, then, do we unbend our bows toward the poor and, instead, more effectively serve those in need? For starters, we must acknowledge that there is no "us versus them." Proverbs 22:2 tells us: "The rich and poor have this in common: The Lord made them both." As Martin Luther King, Jr. stated so eloquently in 1965, "The rich must not ignore the poor because both rich and poor are tied in a single garment of destiny. All life is interrelated, and all men are interdependent."[52]

This interdependence implies that we cannot continue to see poverty as a ministry unto itself, as something we do on a Saturday morning or on holidays. Otherwise, we risk looking down on those who struggle, as Robert D. Lupton pointed out in *Compassion, Justice and the Christian Life,* "as weak ones waiting to be rescued, not bearers of divine treasures." He goes on later in his book: "If we are to rightly care for those in need, the responsibility lies with those with the resources to create systems of exchange built on interdependency rather than dependency."

The responsibility lies with us to create more opportunities, not fewer, for our brothers and sisters to climb out of poverty. To create jobs that empower rather than exploit. To become dear friends with people who do not look like us or earn like us. God precisely calls us to live as neighbors, both relationally and physically, with "widows, orphans, foreigners, and the poor."

Imagine the same boy from earlier, born into a poor family. But instead of being born into an unjust system where he is likely to be trapped in the cycle of poverty, he is born into a compassionate society that views each other as keys to the Kingdom of God. Because we care for each other's future as much as we do our own, his mother is able to afford prenatal care for herself and pediatric care for him. Because we have agreed that every neighborhood deserves to be free from toxic air and water, he is less likely to develop health problems that limit his development.

This young boy will never have to arrive to school hungry, because we have ensured that he always has access to healthy foods. Because he is well-fed, he is alert and more ready to learn. He will learn in a school where he sits side-by-side with other children who may or may not look like him or whose parents earn differently than his own. Parents who advocate for their own children's opportunities will no longer do so at the cost of others' children, but rather they will advocate for the success of all children.

He will never come home to an empty house. Because we understand the importance of present parenthood, we no longer require that his mother work two or more jobs just to pay for rent and food. She will earn the wages we each need to live in a decent and stable home, to have the food we need for today, and to ensure a doctor is available should we need one tomorrow.

This young boy will grow up in a neighborhood that is supportive, where he knows his neighbors, where he will see and know opportunity, and where he will learn from positive role models. In this environment, he is more likely to graduate from high school, go on to complete some form of higher education, and land a stable job.

None of these things are guaranteed, of course. Having healthcare access doesn't mean this young boy will be healthy, and living in a more diverse neighborhood doesn't mean he is immune to bad influences. Having a bigger paycheck will not alone ensure it's spent wisely, and a college education doesn't guarantee he will always have stable, high-paying jobs.

Getting Involved

I once heard someone say that hope without a plan is just a wish. If we hope to overcome the oppression of poverty that entangles millions in America and billions more abroad, we need more than just a wish. We must find a way to get involved.

> "What good is it, dear brothers and sisters, if you say you have faith but don't show it by your actions? Can that kind of faith save anyone? Suppose you see a brother or sister who has no

food or clothing, and you say, 'Good-bye and have a good day; stay warm and eat well'—but then you don't give that person any food or clothing. What good does that do?

"So you see, faith by itself isn't enough. Unless it produces good deeds, it is dead and useless.

"Now someone may argue, 'Some people have faith; others have good deeds.' But I say, 'How can you show me your faith if you don't have good deeds? I will show you my faith by my good deeds.'

"Just as the body is dead without breath, so also faith is dead without good works." (James 2:14-18,26)

Getting involved can take many forms. As an individual, consider opportunities to mentor or tutor youth, helping them grow not only in their academic achievement but also in their social and emotional maturity. When you shop, consider goods that are made by workers who are fairly treated and paid, choosing local options whenever possible. If you have a backyard, consider growing produce that you can donate to a local food bank. And, if you have unused square footage in your home, consider converting that space into an apartment for someone needing a low-cost living option.

As a churchgoer, evaluate your own giving: if you don't yet tithe, consider how you might adjust your budget to make it a priority. If your church community is active in the work of alleviating poverty, commit to joining in that work. If you find that your church is not actively serving the poor in your city, ask leaders how you can partner with them to make a difference.

Pastors and church leaders: the possibilities for using your facility to relieve poverty are countless. Allow neighbors to use your green space as a community garden and agree to cover the cost of water. Open a co-working space whose proceeds could fund job training for those struggling to find or maintain work, and offer space at low or no cost to lower-income entrepreneurs. Consider starting a social enterprise within your space, employing formerly-incarcerated people or other vulnerable populations to operate it.

If you run a business, make serving your employees and your city a priority. Set aside paid time for you and your employees to volunteer at a nonprofit. Find ways to begin sharing your company's proceeds with charitable organizations. Consider removing products from your shelves that are made by companies who exploit their workers. If you don't yet pay your employees a living wage or offer health benefits and paid sick leave, think creatively about how to work toward that goal.

While these suggestions merely scratch the surface of what we can collectively do to lift our neighbors from poverty, they are a start nonetheless. And, as Edward Everett Hale famously said, "I am only one, but I am one. I can't do everything, but I can do something. The something I ought to do, I can do. And by the grace of God, I will."[53]

CHAPTER 9
CULTURE IN FLUX

Almost no one wants to be a fish out of water. I certainly didn't. But when the three of us turned the corner to see the crowd, we immediately recognized our misjudgment. I was leading a small team of college students to teach English in a town outside Osaka, Japan, and during our trip we had the opportunity to attend a traditional Japanese tea festival. Our hosts lent us the attire we needed for the festival—colorful kimonos and wooden slippers. They even took the time to show us how to properly tie the sash around our ceremonial garments.

Imagine our surprise, then, when we arrived at the tea festival to a sea of T-shirts and jeans. I was immediately embarrassed to be the six-foot-two American walking among a crowd of Japanese locals, wearing what felt to me like a bathrobe wrapped in a perfect bow. I had clearly missed a cultural cue.

Naturally, there are plenty of cultural cues I can miss right here at home. As a college freshman in the fall of 2000, a friend gave me a strange look when I asked why so many cars around campus were plastered with white oval-shaped stickers printed with the letters "DMB." Growing up among friends and family who listened to R&B, hip-hop, and pop music, I had barely heard of the Dave Matthews Band, even though by then, they had two top-ten albums and a handful of hit singles under their belt. Of course, the misunderstandings went both ways: my New England classmates considered Maryland to be the "Far South" and wondered aloud if we wore cowboy boots down there (we don't).

What is culture, anyway, that it could lead to embarrassments about kimonos and cowboy boots? Merriam-Webster's dictionary defines culture as "the set of shared attitudes, values, goals, and practices that characterizes an institution or organization."[1] In 1963, John and Ruth Useem defined culture as "the learned and shared behavior of a community of interacting human beings."[2] According to research by the Joshua Project, there are around 17,000 distinct people groups across the globe, each with a unique combination of cultural norms, languages, and ethnic backgrounds[3]. There are about 350 languages spoken in households across the U.S. alone[4].

At some level, each one of us identifies with some elements of culture. Realistically, each person embodies a different combination of cultures to which they've been exposed. My own upbringing exposed me to people, groups, and experiences vastly different from those my wife experienced as a child. Being raised with a Filipino father meant that I would learn to see the world, at least in a small way, the way he saw the world. Living in a majority-minority neighborhood meant that I would be exposed to some of the same food and music and life experiences that my peers were immersed in. In fact, it was not until after high school that I truly understood how unique my cultural experiences actually were, being the white-looking kid from a biracial home in a black neighborhood.

Many aspects of my childhood have shaped the culture I now embody—the way I look at society. The family who lived in the apartment next door to us converted to Islam. The family down the hall had immigrated from Granada. While a few of the kids in my building had skin that looked like mine, many others did not and, even though some of the kids spoke English with an accent, we all got along just the same. Most of the time, anyway.

I got my haircut every four weeks in a dingy, faux-wood paneled barber shop, where the gray-haired barbers spoke to each other in Italian and watched *Young and the Restless* on a TV with a wire hanger antenna. My brother and I would buy knock-off Calvin Klein and Tommy Hilfiger T-shirts from the same store that sold hair weave. My high school's gospel choir, step team, and jazz band each drew larger crowds than the orchestra did. Fried chicken and mumbo sauce served in melting foam clamshells were staples at my neighborhood Chinese carry-outs.

While there's a lot to be nostalgic about when it comes to the culture of my childhood, there was also plenty to lament. In middle school, some of my peers routinely shoplifted from the corner store near our school bus stop, sometimes being chased out of the store by a Pakistani man wielding a golf club. On a regular basis, we would drive by the apartment complex in our neighborhood to find another family's belongings lining the curb after being forcefully evicted. Twice, a home on our block was raided by police for drug activity. A bullet once ricocheted off a street sign, crashing through my parents' bedroom window (gratefully, no one was hurt).

There are positive and negative aspects to every cultural experience, which is why we must be careful not to cling to cultures too tightly. As I stated earlier, we naturally embody aspects of the cultures to which we're exposed; yet, the embodiment of these cultures do not themselves make up our identity. This is crucial to remember for those of us who profess to be Christians, recognizing the ease with which societal norms can become enmeshed with doctrinal beliefs. Across the globe, Christianity is acculturated depending on who the believers are, sometimes creating distortions from what God intended for His people. Stephen Lloyd writes:

> "Christianity is, and from its very inception has been, a cross cultural and diverse religion with no single dominant expression. Throughout history, all Christians have lived in specific cultural contexts, which they have, to varying degrees, embraced and rejected. Regardless of a positive or negative attitude toward their surrounding culture, all Christians must respond to their surrounding context. It is in Christians of many and various responses that Christianity gains its unique multicultural and polyvocal texture as a world religion.

> "Those Christians who embrace surrounding cultures use indigenous language, music, art forms, and rituals as potent resources for their own ends. Christians have a history of taking that which is not Christian, and then filling it with Christian meaning. There are classic examples of this: Christians inherited Roman vestments and German Christmas trees. Yet even at a more basic level, Christians borrow pre-Christian languages and use them for Christian ends. Jesus did not speak Greek, Latin, or English, yet each of those languages has been used to tell his story

and teach his message. As Christianity continues to find a home in new cultural settings, Christians continue to borrow new languages and cultures to tell the story of Jesus."[5]

For example, African American churches grew around the historical experiences of slavery and oppression, emphasizing, as Judith Weisenfeld noted, "biblical narratives like that of the Exodus, which offered them the promise of God's deliverance of his suffering people."[6] Similarly, Latin American churches were influenced by fights against the exploitation by the extremely wealthy in society, leading to what is known as liberation theology[7]. Both black and Latino churches have a history steeped in political activism. On the other hand, predominantly white churches that have evolved from North American and European experiences tend to emphasize personal salvation over common grace and have sought to avoid the integration of religion and politics. That is, until recently.

A Christian Nation?

Even though the advent of Christianity has been traced back to Israel, nearly 1800 years before America became a nation, many consider the United States to be the modern center of Christian culture. Four out of ten Christians believe the U.S. is a Christian nation—and has been so since its founding[8]. Moreover, six out of ten believe "God has granted America a special role in human history," according to a survey by the Public Religion Research Institute[9].

It makes sense why some might feel that way. Even though less than one in five Americans go to church each week, various surveys tell us that about two-thirds of us claim to be Christian[10].

American Christians churn out books and music that sell by the millions, sometimes appealing to an audience that transcends regular churchgoers. Todd Burpo's 2010 book, *Heaven is for Real,* has sold more than 13 million copies to date[11], and its 2014 film adaptation grossed over $100 million at the box office[12]. Christian artists like Lecrae and Lauren Daigle have managed to top *Billboard*'s list of best-selling albums and regularly appear on mainstream talk shows. Christian messaging infiltrates much of popular culture: many of us wear cross necklaces, get praying hands tattooed on our bodies, and watch awards shows sprinkled with celebrity speeches thanking God for their success.

However, Brett McCracken, author and senior editor for The Gospel Coalition, spoke sharply about the conflation between American culture and Christianity:

> "For most of US history, to be *American* was to be 'Christian.' National identity was conflated with religious identity in a way that produced a distorted form of Christianity, mostly about family values, Golden Rule moralism, and good citizenship. The God of this 'Christianity' was first and foremost a nice guy who rewarded moral living by sanctifying the American dream...This faith defined by a distant, 'cosmic ATM' God who only cares that we are nice to one another and feel good about ourselves."[13]

Not surprisingly, McCracken's critique of the Christian-American identity isn't shared by all. In fact, there is a prominent view purported by many well-known evangelicals that America's deep Christian heritage is under attack by secular forces. Dr. Dave Miller, author and Executive Director of

Apologetics Press, says that America is, in fact, a Christian nation facing a war "far more serious and deadly than any physical conflict (like the Iraq war)."[14] In her book *It's Dangerous to Believe*, Mary Eberstadt compares the treatment of Christians today to the Salem witch trials of the late 1600s[15]. In the opening pages of his 2014 book, *God Less America*, Todd Starnes openly accuses then-president Barack Obama of having the goal "to eradicate the Christian faith from the public marketplace of ideas."[16]

Yet, if two out of three Americans identify as Christians, one might wonder why Christians feel as though they are under attack by some groups. Why do American Christians perceive a war on their religion at all, if so many still claim it as their own? In many ways, then, Christians have allowed the dominant culture to affect them in spite of their large numbers and, one might argue, simply increasing the number of Christians in society will not be sufficient to counter that effect.

The Cultural Influence of Christianity

Pastor and author Carey Nieuwhof writes that there are three ways that Christians approach culture poorly[17]. First, Nieuwhof says that Christians can be "oblivious to culture." The people—and their churches—are irrelevant because they are unaware of the cultures around them and are, therefore, unable to relate to them. The second approach to culture, Nieuwhof says, is to hide from it: these folks see culture, but are afraid of it. Instead, these people create "safe" alternatives to the cultural exchanges happening around them, becoming isolated from the people they are supposed to build relationships with. The third, and recently the most popular approach, is to disparage culture: these people see culture as something to be judged for not adopting the dominant Christian morality and, as a result, become ineffective at reaching unchurched people.

To simplify things a bit, I would argue that Christians either affect culture, or are affected by it. And, for the past century or so, it seems the latter has been true.

For centuries, the arts reflected religious themes, with many of the world's most famous works and artists inspired by Christian messaging. Paintings like Leonardo Da Vinci's *The Last Supper*, songs like John Newton's *Amazing Grace*, and cathedrals like Paris' Notre-Dame each had both immediate and lasting impacts on the Western world. It could be said that, in a sense, Christianity created culture. Even the ways in which Christians interacted with society reflected both the eternal and practical nature of the Christian faith, said Gabe Lyons, with evangelism teaching the full gospel trajectory of creation, the fall of man, redemption, and restoration[18].

Beginning in the 19th Century, however, Christian evangelists began to emphasize conversions, focusing only on the fall and redemption portions of the gospel story. These preachers, said Lyons, "didn't have the benefit of living among the people and modeling the life of a Christian over the course of years. Their demanding schedule of traveling by horseback from town to town gave them weeks, and sometimes just days, to convey the depth of the message of Jesus." This, Lyons suggested, is where Christianity began to lose its cultural influence.

If the cultural influence of Christianity is lost in the hustle and bustle of nomadic evangelism, in the shallowness of drive-through relationship, then one could suppose it is regained through immersive community. Much like in mentoring, humans gain credibility and influence by investing in the wellbeing of others, standing alongside them through their successes and failures. Loving them through good times and difficult ones, imparting wisdom along the way. Influence is earned when we transcend our tendency to see others as transactional, seeing them instead as friends in which we invest.

Geography is essential in our human investment. Though we may have hundreds or thousands of "friends" on social media, the depth of our connection with them is limited without proximity. Without the richness of in-person contact, our relationships lack texture, and a cultural filament is lost. A prime example of this is something I've brought up before, which is the way we interact with others when behind the wheel of our vehicles. When we see others as machines that happen to have people inside, rather than as humans moving from place to place, we replace a potentially positive cultural exchange with a poor substitute. If we lose dignified interactions with others to the "virtual" world, we will later lose the dignity of our interactions in the real one.

Culture and the City

When it comes to our built environment, then, it also appears Christians are affected *by* culture more than affectors *of* culture. In his book, *The Imperfect Disciple*, Jared Wilson says, "The message of the suburbs, in a nutshell, is self-empowerment. Self-enhancement. Self-fulfillment...The primary values of suburbia are convenience, abundance, and comfort."[19] Instead of embracing the diversity of God's people, seeking the empowerment of community, and joining forces with other believers in the fight against injustice, many of us have chosen the allures of Eden without any promise of actually achieving it. Instead of green pastures, we have an asphalt landscape dotted with road signs meant to be read at high speeds, lawns that serve only to delineate the realm of one man over another, and houses that are more symbols of personal success than harbors of hospitality.

Recently, I attended a conference where TV screens were staged throughout the convention center, showing a rotation of short videos highlighting small cities and towns across America. They were bedroom communities of larger cities, really, where housing is plentiful but jobs are not, and the typical homeowner spends a significant chunk of their day commuting for work. These were more promotional videos than documentaries, though, with mayors and city managers selling viewers on their cities' safety and "good" schools. I was struck by the way in which leader after leader would use *safe* and *good schools* in the same sentence, implying that these features alone are the hallmarks of a good community and, subversively, that their "competitors" don't offer these features.

The mayors and city managers in the videos, of course, have a duty to advocate for their communities, much like any other CEO would promote his or her company. I certainly wouldn't expect them to highlight their long commutes or lack of industry. It is normal to want a neighborhood that is safe and has access to quality education. But the coded language I heard reflects an anti-urban bias that is not just outdated, but also rooted in a deeply racist past. In part, our suburban neighborhoods and bedroom communities are safe because we've fled the scene. Our suburban schools have high test scores not because our children are more intelligent or better behaved, but because we facilitate a system where suburban schools are funded at higher levels than urban ones, sending signals about which children are valued more and which are not[20].

The Bible encourages Christians to settle our cities, supporting their peace and prosperity. In Jeremiah 29, we read a message from God to a group of people who have been exiled to

Babylon from Jerusalem:

> "Build homes, and plan to stay. Plant gardens, and eat the food they produce. Marry and have children. Then find spouses for them so that you may have many grandchildren. Multiply! Do not dwindle away! And work for the peace and prosperity of the city where I sent you into exile. Pray to the Lord for it, for its welfare will determine your welfare." (Jeremiah 29:5-7)

To affect culture in the context of our cities, then, requires that we develop them, sow into them, raise families in them, and advocate for the wellbeing of each person within them. Otherwise, we risk being affected by a culture that is luring us into a security that is only skin deep.

Some Christians may see this call to settlement as in conflict with other scriptures about our alienness here on earth. After all, the Bible is clear that believers are strangers in this world. The apostle Paul calls us "citizens of heaven" in Philippians 3:20. Another apostle, Peter, calls us "foreigners" in 1 Peter 2:11. But I see the relationship as less of a conflict and more of a healthy tension. Our investment in the physical should be aligned, culturally, with our investment in the spiritual. Known by theologians as the "already but not yet" concept, the Kingdom of God is seen as a realm that exists presently on earth as well as in the future in heaven. In fact, the exile of the Israelites in Jeremiah 29, who were instructed not just to camp out but to make Babylon like their home, might serve as a roadmap for Christians on earth today.

Beautiful Places

Not just about peace, prosperity, or the pursuit of justice, consideration of our place in culture is also about beauty. In the same way that we are drawn to the beauty of nature, we also flock to the beauty that results from man's God-given creativity. It is no secret that we assign higher value to places we see as beautiful. The iconic Painted Ladies of San Francisco are some of the most photographed houses in the world, lining the Bay Area's streetscape with colorful Victorian architecture. New York City's Times Square attracts a staggering 130 million visitors each year, aweing pedestrians with its dizzying array of digital billboards and street performers[21]. The Eiffel Tower, once considered an eyesore by Parisians, is now one of the most famous landmarks in the world, ground zero for many marriage proposals over its 130-year history. In fact, more than 1.5 billion people travel internationally each year to experience places like the winding streets of Stockholm's Old Town, the metallic sheen of Bilbao's Guggenheim museum, and the quiet grandeur of Mount Vernon[22].

Beyond the world's most iconic tourist attractions, beautiful places attract people more than other places do. People gather in farmers markets, town squares, plazas, and even on crowded main streets when they are framed by attractive streetscapes. Here in San Antonio, our most popular farmers markets are not the ones that crop up in strip mall parking lots, but in places like the Pearl, a walkable, mixed-use district repurposed from an old brewery that was designed with careful attention to detail. In fact, the Pearl was awarded the Great Places designation in 2017 by the American Planning Association because of its quality streetscapes and family-friendly programming[23]. It happens to be home to Hotel Emma, ranked by numerous publications as one of the best hotels in America and the world[24].

The Church in Context

In places like Italy, Armenia, Bulgaria, and Egypt, early Christian churches were designed with a strong architectural presence. The cultural influence of the early church was so strong, in fact, that these sanctuaries were usually sited at the center of town, visible from nearly every vantage point of the community. This was not only true of historic European and northern African cities, but also of Colonial-era U.S. cities like Annapolis and Philadelphia. The addition of the steeple to Christ Church in Philadelphia made it the tallest structure in North America until Boston's Park Street Church was completed in 1810[25]. And, although New York City is now known for its fabric of skyscrapers, Trinity Church remained the tallest building in the city from its completion in 1846 until 1890[26].

Much of this attention to architecture and sense of place dissipated with the rise of suburbia, and the cultural centers of our communities shifted from civic and religious buildings to commercial ones. As the church's place in culture shifted, so did its emphasis on architecture. Protestantism became characterized by what urban analyst Aaron Renn calls, "worldly pragmatism," with its buildings lacking any real symbolic purpose except to serve as a place to gather in worship[27]. Non-denominational churches tend "to see the spiritual as distinct from the physical, with the true Christian life being inward and spiritual." This has led to what Renn calls "aesthetic neglect," with modern-day churches adapting to the contemporary culture of consumerism. These buildings emphasize cheap construction, spending more instead on production and programming. As a result, the exteriors of today's churches are indistinguishable from those of schools, shopping centers, or office buildings.

All of this is not to disparage churches that meet in unadorned buildings. As I concluded in Chapter 5, it's not whether a church is big or small (or, in this case, beautiful or boring) that matters, but whether or not it fosters and strengthens the community. My own church, in fact, started in what used to be a tire shop. But, when the architecturally significant church buildings are no longer inhabited by an actual church community, others are quick to fill the void, repurposing those sacred spaces as museums, hotels or, in a recent case here in San Antonio, a restaurant that sold gourmet hot dogs. The place had become affectionately known as "hot dog church."

How does the American Church, collectively, transition from a tradition of nomadic evangelism to a state of immersive community, especially in a culture that celebrates both wanderlust and stasis? Is it even possible to build community-serving churches in a society that's willing to drive to whichever church fits its wish list? Think about the largest churches in your own city—it's possible you even attend one of them. Would you want one of those churches to be located on your street?

It may seem as though we are far removed from the days of the central church, where our civic and religious buildings are surrounded by the homes and businesses of our communities. But churches that fully understand the gospel will seek, as Timothy Keller writes in *Center Church*, "the welfare of the city, neighborhood and civic involvement, cultural engagement, and training people to work in 'secular' vocations out of a Christian worldview." These churches will approach culture not with fear or total assimilation, but with what is known as *contextualization*. Keller writes:

"Contextualization is not—as is often argued—
giving people what they want to hear. Rather, it
is giving people the Bible's answers, which they
may not at all want to hear, to questions about life
that people in their particular time and place are
asking, in language and forms they can comprehend, and through appeals and arguments with
force they can feel, even if they reject them."

Contextualization, then, is about serving the local community with the complete gospel in a way that considers rather
than dismisses the local culture. Keller goes on to describe why
churches should be intentional about contextualization:

"There are five million new people moving into
the cities of the developing world every month—
roughly the size of the metropolitan areas of
Philadelphia or San Francisco...how many
churches ought there to be in a city the size of
Philadelphia?...The people of the world are now
moving into the great cities of the world many
times faster than the church is...The growth in
size and influence of cities today presents the
greatest possible challenge for the church. Never
before has it been so important to learn how to do
effective ministry in cities, and yet, by and large,
evangelical Christianity in the United States is
still nonurban."

The implication here is that churches remaining on the
sidelines of culture are, in essence, being affected by it. Or,
perhaps more importantly, in an increasingly urbanizing world,
a dominant suburban American church may only decrease in

its cultural relevance. As I highlighted at the beginning of the chapter, there are as many as 17,000 distinct people groups living on every corner of our planet, each with a unique culture. In light of the Great Commission, which tells Christians to "make disciples of all the nations,"—which truly means to reach every one of those 17,000 people groups—how can we truly do this if we are not intentional about engaging culture? "If we are not deliberately thinking about our culture," Keller says, "we will simply be conformed to it without ever knowing it is happening." I would argue that this conforming is already happening, and has been for a long time.

—

As families and churches embraced the shift to suburbia, another cultural response has emerged in our communities. Especially true of our older neighborhoods is what I call the born-and-raised bias—the belief that simply being from a place or having remained in that place for a long time is a source of credibility not "earned" by those who arrived more recently. We see this bias in local politics, where candidates for elected office tout their birthplace as an advantage over their opponents. It is prevalent in urban planning efforts, where long-time residents are presumed to know best when it comes to the future of their communities, and newcomers are viewed with skepticism. It even creeps into our national discourse about immigration, with many people judging others' "Americanness" by how many generations have passed since their families first arrived on our shores.

Perhaps part of why Western Christians—and the Church as a whole—have struggled with its approach to culture is that our role within it can feel dissonant. If we are honest with ourselves, we will recognize that many of the norms we live out in our daily lives are, in fact, shaped by the cultures of where we live. At the same time, actively living out the commands given to us within the gospel of Christ is incredibly countercultural. This dissonance plays out in very tangible ways across our nation.

To see culture rightly is not to pretend it doesn't exist, preferring some parallel culture that offers little to the world. Neither is it to deride culture, judging its adherents for claiming a different morality than that of the majority of Christians. As author and church-planting coach Dan White, Jr. said, "fighting a culture war was never the commission given to the Church."[28] If America's culture, and the culture of the West in general, is in flux, the only effective way to influence culture is to embed one's self in the creation of it. For some, culture creation will result in big endeavors like writing books, creating inspiring films, and making beautiful music. Others will teach and research in academia, or design structures that will change our landscapes for the better. Yet, culture is also built in the everyday. Invite a neighbor over for dinner, even if the invitation feels awkward. Bring a carafe of coffee to your office and invite coworkers for a cup, using the opportunity to get to know them. Or, as author Alan Briggs highlighted in his book *Staying is the New Going*, set up that carafe in your front yard, welcoming neighbors and other passers-by for a drink.

CHAPTER 10
EMBRACE THE CIRCLE

Elephants are pretty smart creatures. Despite their enormous size, they are still considered prey to lions. When a herd senses a lion has come around to try and take down one of them for lunch (and probably leftovers), the elephants do something pretty incredible. They form a circle, each adult elephant facing outward, and hide their young in the center. Each attempt by the lion to take them out is thwarted by a swift swat from their trunks, frustrating the lion and eventually causing him to hang back.

In one of these scenarios, caught on film by wildlife videographers, one of the smaller elephants decided to take off running. For no discernable reason, this elephant abandoned the herd and, without hesitation, the lion attacked that lone elephant, leading to his demise.

Matt Carter, pastor of The Austin Stone Community Church, points us to 1 Peter 5:8, revealing the parallel between this herd of elephants and our own human nature: "Stay alert! Watch out for your great enemy, the devil. He prowls around like a roaring lion, looking for someone to devour." Carter emphasizes the word *someone*, recognizing that we humans are more susceptible to our enemies in isolation than we are when we bond together in community[1].

"Satan is not in a hurry to take you out." Carter says. "He's patient...and he waits until a believer, a Christian, isolates himself from other Christians—removes himself from community. And, that is when he pounces."

Carter concludes, "Satan's trophy room is full of Christians that thought they could live the Christian life apart from community."

Enduring graduate school early in my marriage was a challenge for me and my wife. Just two years into being husband and wife, we moved to a city that neither of us particularly liked, she took a job that tested her limits, and my full-time work routine was interrupted by long hours of classes, papers, and two part-time jobs. I settled deep into my frustration, eventually reaching a place where I had given up. I had announced to my wife that I was done trying. I wanted out of our marriage.

What happened next forever changed me, and forever changed our relationship. My wife reached out to our church for help, and like a herd of heart-filled elephants, they circled around us. A man from our church's small group called me, imploring me that I would stay and give my marriage a chance. Another couple we knew began meeting with us on a regular basis, walking us through Dr. Emerson Eggerich's *Love & Respect*, a book we continue to recommend to couples to this day. We shifted our routines in order to focus on the health of our marriage, and years later I can honestly say my wife and I are stronger together than ever.

Often, when we recognize others going through a tough time, and especially through a tough season in their relationship, we think the best thing to do is to give them space. "I'm here if you need anything," we might say. But, I would argue that sitting in wait is not enough. Forming a circle to stand against our enemies requires our action. Keeping our neighbors from danger means leading them to places that are safe from attack.

—

For nearly a decade, I thought I wanted to become an architect. Throughout my childhood I sketched out floor plans of homes I wanted to build—sometimes for myself, sometimes for others. I had folders filled with drawings, many of which would make absolutely no sense as a real house. I pored through furniture catalogs, memorizing the common dimensions of sofas, dining tables, and beds. As a class project, I built a scale model of Mount Vernon—so successfully, in fact, that it was kept in my middle school library for years afterward.

Yet, when I finally made it to architecture school, I quickly figured out that something wasn't right. As I sat in the studio for many hours each week, stressing over how I might please my professors by designing some abstract exhibit space, or by proving I understood concepts like *repetition* and *rhythm*, I knew a degree in architecture wasn't for me. I handed in my drafting supplies and never looked back.

For some of you, this book may be a call to that kind of change. It might mean coming to terms with the reality that the suburban experiment has failed you in some way: the sense of community it promised has fostered isolation instead; the freedom of the open road was a lie, instead delivering hours of congestion and a host of unexpected costs; and the heterogeneity of your neighborhood dilutes the gospel's message of inclusion. This change could mean an intentional change of address, a migration toward the city. Embracing a smaller footprint to be in the presence of footprints made by every walk of life.

For others of you, a move from the suburbs isn't practical—and that's okay. The suburbs aren't going away anytime soon, and that serves as an opportunity. Staying put is a chance to contribute to the culture of your community, to engage with your neighbors, to put away the car keys from time to time, and to embrace the good that exists in your own neighborhood. It means having the opportunity to minister to people who feel isolated, frazzled, or unable to keep up with the demands this life has made on them. It means demanding better buildings and safer streets from your local elected officials.

If you pastor a church or serve in one, this message can be both really encouraging and really frustrating. Embracing the circle is a strong message for building community that gathers beyond weekend services. But, if you happen to shepherd a highway-church, one characterized more by its exit number than its neighborhood, it can be really difficult to counter that reality. Changing church locations isn't easy or cheap, and can really prove challenging in the face of a congregation who has grown used to traveling by car to attend your services. In fact, you may find yourself struggling with how to meet the needs of commuters by adding parking to your facility without encouraging the negative externalities that come with it.

Embracing the circle is not just a call to live or worship in the city, though I think many of us would benefit a great deal from taking that leap of faith. It is about answering the call to live as though we are each linked together in a circle, with no one at the head or the foot of the table. It means recognizing that my decisions impact you, and your decisions impact me. The urban life depends on the rural, and the rural on the urban. A life in America relates to one's life in Albania, Argentina, or Austria.

Every dollar we earn and spend affects those earned and spent by our neighbors, whether we realize it or not.

It means understanding the human cost of not just how we live, or how we consume, but also *where*. Embracing the circle will mean we pursue a better built environment, and not just because there is value in the aesthetic of place. We will seek to build and evolve communities that ensure our planet is healthy for our children and their children, for our neighbors here and abroad. We will empower neighborhoods that promote justice by acting on behalf of the poor in our midst and joyfully sharing our wealth to benefit others. We will not simply be affected by the most dominant voices in culture, but we will create a culture in alignment with God's character and His vision for His people.

This will necessitate some hard questions for you and for me. Will we accept living in a neighborhood where all my neighbors look or earn as I do? Is it ethical for us to demand the funded maintenance and expansion of a transportation system that results in the lost lives of tens of thousands each year? Does it reflect Christ that our fast life—one of fast food, fast fashion, and fast furniture—comes cheaply to us at the cost of others' health and livelihood? Will our churches preach the gospel of Christ, steeped richly in love for God and neighbor, or will they preach a gospel of independence and personal prosperity?

Even as I look around my living room right now, I am overwhelmed at the thought of what my consumer choices are bringing about in this world. The cotton woven into my sofa fabric was surely treated with pesticides, sprayed by a farmer who could very well see long-term impacts to his health. The television contains metals mined in its manufacture and will continue to impact this planet once the TV no longer functions in a few years. The synthetic area rug beneath my feet is made with the very same crude oil that fuels our cars, soaked in dyes that may still be off-gassing to this day, and produced by someone forced to inhale those toxic fumes in their daily work. The wood harvested to make my side table and the art piece on my wall have sapped yet another source of clean air and flood mitigation from a family now more vulnerable overseas. All of it was packaged in foams and plastics that will stuff our landfills and float in our oceans for thousands of years.

As desperate as all of this sounds, there is another way. It will require us to look around our circle, and learn to recognize the human beings who make up our lives, each and every one created in the image of God. It requires the acknowledgment that there is no such thing as a self-made man, but rather a man or woman who is linked arm-in-arm with all those who make their growth and success possible. Your career doesn't exist without your customers, and your customers don't exist without their careers. Your education is incomplete without your teachers, and your teachers are not teachers without their education. Where you live is not built in a vacuum, either; it requires thousands of parts that are mined, manufactured, mixed, cut up and joined together, all by people who have lives just like we do.

There are six ways we can learn to embrace the circle, ways we can begin practically changing our environment to benefit others, our planet, and our own future.

1. Rethink your home. Learning what truly brings you joy about your home can really help you hone in on what it is you actually need. As I've written throughout this book, we have made many mindless assumptions about what is best for us in a place to live. Does a backyard really add value to my life, or is it more of an obligation? Does a guest bedroom really make sense for me, or is that square footage sucking up money and energy that could be best used elsewhere? Is my home's square footage the problem, or is it that its layout doesn't work well for my needs? Do I truly need a home that's physically separated from others, or am I really craving more access to nature? Are my cabinets and closets filled with things I actually use, or could I honestly do without some of what's there?

2. Rethink your commute. Sometimes we need to be reminded that the best way to move from place to place is the way we have always moved: on our feet. Walking, riding our bicycles, and taking public transportation have numerous benefits that outweigh what we think we've gained by driving alone. Am I already close enough to the office to walk or bike there? Can I use public transit to get to work without sacrificing much more of my day? What are the things I would rather be doing than driving? Can I do any of those things by walking, biking, or riding transit? Have I stopped to consider rearranging some things to take advantage of a shorter commute, like changing pharmacies, finding a different day care center, or using a nearby co-working space once or twice a week instead of going into the office? Could my commute be made less stressful by sharing it with someone else who works near me?

3. Rethink your neighborhood. For thousands of years, our communities were what we call mixed-use today: residents would easily walk from their homes to get food, to gather in worship, to trade goods, and to engage in the arts. The private and public realms were necessarily nearby. As the growth of industry led to the increased pollution of our air and water, we over-corrected, separating ourselves from all the other functions

of a healthy city. Could our lives be improved by allowing the
functionality of our places to "recluster" together? What might
we gain by demanding neighborhoods where our children
can once again walk to school and to the park, where we can
walk or bike to access healthy foods, where the family doctor is
blocks—rather than miles—away? What might it mean for the
Christian witness if we routinely love our neighbors—the ones
we encounter routinely as we go about our daily lives?

4. Rethink your church. Stay calm, pastors. This is not
a suggestion that churchgoers find a new place to worship. I
believe it is deeper than that. You see, the suburbanization of
America embedded in our psyches the idea that we should shop
for a church the way we shop for clothes: to find a place that
makes us feel comfortable, that plays the music we like best and
that, more or less, says what we want to hear each week. What
if, instead, we chose a church home based on how we can best
serve it? Or based on how we can best engage in community
with others, including those who are not like us? Does your
church actively seek to reach the local community, including
all the diversity it offers? Does your church empower you to do
more than just attend on Sunday? Does it stretch you and make
you grow as a person?

5. Rethink your stuff. There isn't just something for
everyone anymore: there's something for every*thing*. It seems
that almost everything we buy isn't complete unless we buy
something else for it. We buy covers and screen protectors for
our phones. We buy organizers for our refrigerators. We buy
contraptions to keep clothes from falling off our hangers. Our
lives are filled with single-purpose objects we could probably

do well without: avocado slicers, baby wipe warmers, cufflinks, automated dog treat dispensers, and on and on it goes. Some out there have admirably downsized their belongings to keep within a set of parameters, like the *100 Thing Challenge* made popular by author Dave Bruno[2]. Through that challenge, people like Bruno have opted to live with no more than 100 personal possessions. While a task of that magnitude could be intimidating for most of us, seriously considering what possessions we truly need could be liberating.

6. Rethink your neighbors. In a society that encourages the meticulous curation of our lives—we curate our music and television content on streaming services, we curate our meals by eating out more and more, and we curate our homes by scrolling endlessly through websites like Pinterest and Houzz—we have fallen into the trap of also curating our neighbors. We can choose our neighborhood and our friends no differently than we choose where to vacation. What if, instead, we risked getting to know the people around us? The ones older or younger than we are. The ones with children or the still childless. The ones with darker or lighter skin. The ones who seem more intellectual or who seem less educated. The ones who talk too much or who barely say a word. The ones full of tattoos or full of themselves. Jim Wallis' statement bears repeating that "there are no 'nonneighbors' in this world."

Just this morning I came face to face with my own inadequacy when it comes to embracing the circle. As I arrived at a coffee shop before sunrise, ready to study the bible with other men from my church, a young man named Felix sat down with me, still in his work uniform. I explained that several of my friends would be arriving soon and that I would be using the table. But he sat down anyway. I made small talk with him, hoping that he would eventually get the message that this was *our* table. As the rest of the guys showed up, crowding around the table, Felix remained there, silent. To be completely honest, I felt as though he was intruding.

But then something happened. I could see that Felix would occasionally look up from the game he was playing on his phone, listening in as we talked through Paul's letter to the Ephesians. Finally, one of the guys from my group asked Felix for his thoughts about what we'd been discussing, and he shared some of his story with us. Over the next ten minutes, I was moved by Felix's story of journeying through homelessness and, at the same time, saddened by my own selfishness. How can I truly embrace the circle without being willing to expand it?

You see, we are more than just the flesh and bone sitting where we are right now. We are more than even the souls inside us, vying for meaning here on earth. We are sons and daughters, brothers and sisters, husbands and wives, fathers and mothers, friends and strangers, all woven together in a crown of God's creation. In this reality, we are not just mysteriously alive, but we are part of God's mysterious Kingdom. His circle.

Our influence doesn't just end with ourselves, our families, or our closest friends. Through God's power alone, our reach is literally endless. Ephesians 4:3-4 tells us, "Make every effort to keep yourselves united in the Spirit, binding yourselves together with peace. For there is one body and one Spirit, just as you have been called to one glorious hope for the future."

This is the case for faith in cities. As we bind together as peacemakers through Jesus, we reflect His character to others among us in the places we inhabit. My hope is that you now have faith that it is in our cities where we are most empowered to do that.

Acknowledgments

Writing a book is not glamorous. Some days the ideas flow, and other days you struggle to find the strength to keep going. Pushing past busyness and insecurity can be a messy process, and I am grateful to everyone who kept me going these last four years and helped make this project possible. You all are a gift.

Brent, I don't think this book would have seen the light of day without you. Thank you for keeping me on course when other voices were steering me astray. Your friendship, your leadership, and your unique perspective are much appreciated. I still can't believe the trust you put in Tara and me to partner with you in ministry.

Olivia Quintana, thank you for your generosity and attention to detail. Your edits absolutely made this project worthy of print. And, to my beta readers, thanks so much for spending quality time reading and giving your honest feedback. Sara Joy Proppe, Rick Archer, Jonathan Malm, and Drew Smith, you are all incredible.

Cristian Ortiz-Salas, thanks for making me look better than I do in real life. Your photography and design skills are truly one-of-a-kind.

A special thanks to everyone who contributed their stories

and perspectives to this project: Reward Sibanda, Nathan Hunt, Andrew Moore, Michael Watkins, Chris & Melissa Bruntlett, and Adrian Crook.

And, because this book can't happen without the encouragement of friends, colleagues, and family, thanks to everyone who inspired and pushed me throughout this process. There are far too many of you to print your names here and, for that, I feel incredibly rich.

Last, and certainly not least, thank you to my amazing wife. Tara, your love and patience make me better and without you none of this would be possible.

NOTES

Chapter 1

[1]GSS Data Explorer. "Can people be trusted." NORC at the University of Chicago. https://gssdataexplorer.norc.org/variables/441/vshow

[2]United States Crime Rates 1960-2018. http://www.disastercenter.com/crime/uscrime.htm

[3]Dilmaghani, Maryam. 2017. "Religiosity and Social Trust: Evidence from Canada." *Review of Social Economy* 75 (1): 49–75. doi:10.1080/00346764.2016.1186820.

[4]Traunmüller, Richard. 2011. "Moral Communities? Religion as a Source of Social Trust in a Multilevel Analysis of 97 German Regions." *European Sociological Review* 27 (3): 346-363. doi:10.1093/esr/jcq011

Welch, M.R., Sikkink, D., Sartain, E., Bond, C., 2004. Trust in God and trust in man: the ambivalent role of religion in shaping dimensions of social trust. *Journal for the Scientific Study of Religion* 43, 317–343.

[5]Berggren, Niclas, and Christian Bjørnskov. "Does religiosity promote or discourage social trust? Evidence from cross-country and cross-state comparisons." *Evidence from Cross-Country and Cross-State Comparisons* (October 10, 2009) (2009).

[6]Pew Research Center, Nov. 3, 2015, "U.S. Public Becoming Less Religious."

[7]Daniels, Alex. 2013. "Religious Americans Give More, New Study Finds." The Chronicle of Philanthropy. https://www.philanthropy.com/article/Religious-Americans-Give-More/153973

[8]Steffan, Melissa. 2013. "Who Volunteers the Most?" Christianity Today. https://www.christianitytoday.com/ct/2013/may/who-volunteers-most.html

[9]AAA Newsroom. 2016. "Nearly 80 Percent of Drivers Express Significant Anger, Aggression or Road Rage." AAA Foundation for Traffic Safety. https://newsroom. aaa.com/2016/07/nearly-80-percent-of-drivers-express-significant-anger-aggression-or-road-rage/

[10]Interview with Mark Dever and Jim Wallis. 2010. "Personal but Never Private" Christianity Today. https://www.christianitytoday.com/pastors/2010/summer/personalneverprivate.html

[11]Wirzba, Norman. 2016. "Is Christian Faith a Private Matter?" The Huffington Post. https://www.huffpost.com/entry/is-christian-faith-a-priv_b_9284910?-guccounter=1&guce_referrer=aHR0cHM6Ly93d3cuZ29vZ2xlLmNvbS88&-guce_referrer_sig=AQAAAAUQqCIjd5QzuSc6FvEiVMVjK1-G-aHzWw9QTL-J2uH_31bL4gB1DRGMb-BRWJmdRgEDvsb7k--44vT91NukmvG7VKpycok-8jLKckT1NegoySndl0Plwx6pA99sDaEuqqyd2dHQ4Os4aqsF_XZTPRPM-Km8-4I3FywuWas4Y51KNgQ

[12]UNHCR, The UN Refugee Agency. https://www.unhcr.org/en-us/syria-emergency.html

Chapter 2

[1]Snyder, Mike. 2017. "Perceived link between transit, crime tough to dispel." Houston Chronicle. https://www.houstonchronicle.com/news/columnists/greater-houston/article/Perceived-link-between-transit-crime-tough-to-11303477.php

[2]O'Brien Cailin. 2014. "Clayton County gives MARTA input on first bus routes." Clayton News-Daily. https://www.news-daily.com/news/clayton-county-gives-marta-input-on-first-bus-routes/article_ee9d3ec8-b8cf-512d-908f-0cf73367c775.html

[3]Obrinsky, Mark and Stein, Debra. 2007. "Overcoming Opposition to Multifamily Rental Housing." Joint Center for Housing Studies, Harvard University. https://www.jchs.harvard.edu/sites/default/files/rr07-14_obrinsky_stein.pdf

[4]Young, Cheryl. 2016. "There Doesn't Go the Neighborhood: Low-Income Housing Has No Impact on Nearby Home Values." Trulia. https://www.trulia.com/research/low-income-housing/

[5]PK. 2019. "Historical Homeownership Rate in the United States, 1890-Present." DQYDJ. https://dqydj.com/historical-homeownership-rate-in-the-united-states-1890-present/

[6]Wheelock, David C. 2008. "The Federal Response to Home Mortgage Distress: Lessons from the Great Depression." Federal Reserve Bank of St. Louis Review. https://files.stlouisfed.org/files/htdocs/publications/review/08/05/Wheelock.pdf

[7]O'Toole, Randal. 2012 "American Nightmare: How Government Undermines the Dream of Homeownership." Cato Institute.

[8]"The Most Perfectly Planned Community in America!" promotional brochure, Levittown Collection.

[9]"We'll be Inside...Looking Out!" advertisement in LIFE Magazine, February 19, 1945.

[10]National Association of Realtors. 2018. "Quick Real Estate Statistics." https://www.nar.realtor/research-and-statistics/quick-real-estate-statistics

[11]"New Residential Construction: Historical Data" 2019. United States Census Bureau. https://www.census.gov/construction/nrc/historical_data/index.html

[12]"Historical Census of Housing Tables." 2011. United States Census Bureau, Housing and Household Economic Statistics Division. https://www.census.gov/hhes/www/housing/census/historic/units.html

[13]Muresan, Adela. 2016. "Who Lives Largest? The Growth of Urban American Homes in the Last 100 Years." Property Shark. https://www.propertyshark.com/Real-Estate-Reports/2016/09/08/the-growth-of-urban-american-homes-in-the-last-100-years/

[14]Clark, Patrick. 2016. "America is Building More Three-Car Garages Than One-Bedroom Apartments." Bloomberg. https://www.bloomberg.com/news/articles/2016-10-26/you-ll-never-be-homeless-in-america-if-you-re-a-car

[15]Collins, William J., and Robert A. Margo. 2011. "Race and Home Ownership from the End of the Civil War to the Present." *American Economic Review*, 101(3): 355-59.

[16]"Understanding Fair Housing." 1973. U.S. Commission on Civil Rights. https://www2.law.umaryland.edu/marshall/usccr/documents/cr11042.pdf

[17]McMullen, Troy. 2019. "The 'heartbreaking' decrease in black homeownership." The Washington Post. https://www.washingtonpost.com/news/business/wp/2019/02/28/feature/the-heartbreaking-decrease-in-black-homeownership/

[18]"Historical Shift from Explicit to Implicit Policies Affecting Housing Segregation in Eastern Massachusetts: 1968-Present: Housing Discrimination." The Fair Housing Center of Greater Boston. https://www.bostonfairhousing.org/timeline/1968-Housing-Discrimination-Today.html

[19]See 17.

[20]Badger, Emily. 2016. "This can't happen by accident." The Washington Post: The Divided American Dream. https://www.washingtonpost.com/graphics/business/wonk/housing/atlanta/

[21]Fry, Richard and Taylor, Paul. 2012. "The Rise of Residential Segregation by Income." Pew Research Center. https://www.pewsocialtrends.org/2012/08/01/the-rise-of-residential-segregation-by-income/

[22]"The 2016 Distressed Communities Index: An Analysis of Community Well-Being Across the United States." Economic Innovation Group. https://eig.org/wp-content/uploads/2016/02/2016-Distressed-Communities-Index-Report.pdf

[23]Reardon, S.F., & Bischoff K. 2016. "The Continuing Increase in Income Segregation, 2007-2012." Stanford Center for Education Policy Analysis. http://cepa.stanford.edu/content/continuing-increase-income-segregation-2007-2012

[24]Unified Development Code. 2020. Municode. https://library.municode.com/tx/san_antonio/codes/unified_development_code

[25]Ratner, Michael and Glover, Carol. 2014. U.S. Energy: Overview and Key Statistics. Congressional Research Service. https://fas.org/sgp/crs/misc/R40187.pdf

[26]Frakt, Austin. 2019. "Stuck and Stressed: The Health Costs of Traffic." *The New York Times*. https://www.nytimes.com/2019/01/21/upshot/stuck-and-stressed-the-health-costs-of-traffic.html

[27]Ogden, Cynthia L. and Carroll, Margaret D. 2010. "Prevalence of Overweight, Obesity, and Extreme Obesity Among Adults, Trends 1960-1962 Through 2007-2008." Center for Disease Control National Center for Health Statistics. https://www.cdc.gov/nchs/data/hestat/obesity_adult_07_08/obesity_adult_07_08.pdf

[28]Albert Henry, Tanya. 2018. "Adult obesity rates rise in 6 states, exceed 35% in 7." American Medical Association. https://www.ama-assn.org/delivering-care/public-health/adult-obesity-rates-rise-6-states-exceed-35-7

[29]Thompson, David. 2013. "Suburban Sprawl: Exposing Hidden Costs, Identifying Innovations." Smart Prosperity Institute. https://institute.smartprosperity.ca/content/cost-sprawl

[30]Steinberger, Alex. 2018. "Fiscal Impact of Residential Development." Fregonese Associates. https://www.sanantonio.gov/Portals/0/Files/NHSD/Housing/FiscalImpactsResidential_FinalReport_031218.pdf

Chapter 3

[1]Ehrenhalt, Alan. 2013. *The Great Inversion and the Future of the American City*.

[2]Imagine Waco: A Plan for Greater Downtown. 2010. Fregonese & Associates. https://prosperwaco.org/app/uploads/Downtown-Masterplan-2010.pdf

[3]Schechter, David. 2019. "Verify: Do Chip and Joanna Gaines get more visitors than the Alamo?" WFAA-TV. https://www.wfaa.com/article/news/verify/verify-do-chip-and-joanna-gaines-get-more-visitors-than-the-alamo/287-b2126906-063b-432b-9b80-9dd27ef74de8

[4]Chen, Crystal. 2019. "New York City Neighborhood Rent Map (Summer 2019)." Zumper. https://www.zumper.com/blog/2019/07/new-york-city-neighborhood-rent-map-summer-2019/

[5]"San Francisco, CA Rental Market Trends." 2019. Yardi Systems. https://www.rentcafe.com/average-rent-market-trends/us/ca/san-francisco/

[6]McDonald, Emily. 2018. "Park Slope Lands Among 10 Priciest NYC Nabes for the First Time." One Block Over, StreetEasy. https://streeteasy.com/blog/park-slope-prices-hit-record-q1-2018-market-reports/

[7]Redfin. https://www.redfin.com/OR/Portland/633-NW-11th-Ave-97209/home/26654826

[8]Olick, Diana. 2015. "High rents trickle down to smaller cities." CNBC. https://www.cnbc.com/2015/02/19/high-rents-trickle-down-to-smaller-cities.html

[9]Moskowitz, Peter. 2015. "The two Detroits: a city both collapsing and gentrifying at the same time." *The Guardian*. https://www.theguardian.com/cities/2015/feb/05/detroit-city-collapsing-gentrifying

[10]Shivani, Anis. 2014. "How oligarchs destroyed a major American city." *Salon*. https://www.salon.com/2014/11/28/how_oligarchs_destroyed_a_major_american_city_partner/

[11]Newkirk II, Vann. "Irrigating the (Food) Desert: A Tale of Gentrification in D.C." *Gawker*. https://gawker.com/irrigating-the-food-desert-a-tale-of-gentrification-1617679708

[12]Cortright, Joe and Mahmoudi, Dillon. 2014. "Lost in Place: Why the persistence and spread of concentrated poverty—not gentrification—is our biggest urban challenge." *City Observatory*. http://cityobservatory.org/wp-content/uploads/2014/12/LostinPlace_12.4.pdf

[13]Riggs, Deidra. 2015. "Gentrification, Redemption, and the Kingdom of God." The High Calling. https://www.theologyofwork.org/the-high-calling/blog/gentrification-redemption-and-kingdom-god

[14]Molina, April. 2018. "Henry Cisneros gives tour of inequality crisis and hope for affordable housing." WOAI. https://news4sanantonio.com/news/local/henry-cisneros-gives-tour-of-inequality-crisis-and-hope-for-affordable-housing

[15]Schwarz, Benjamin. 2010. "Gentrification and its Discontents." *The Atlantic.* https://www.theatlantic.com/magazine/archive/2010/06/gentrification-and-its-discontents/308092/

[16]Repair Priorities 2014: Transportation spending strategies to save taxpayer dollars and improve roads. 2014. Smart Growth America. https://www.smartgrowthamerica.org/app/legacy/documents/repair-priorities-2014.pdf

[17]Jaffe, Eric. 2016. "12 of America's Biggest Highway Boondoggles." *CityLab.* https://www.citylab.com/transportation/2016/01/highway-boondoggle-uspirg/424700/

[18]Garnham, Juan Pablo. 2019. "Texas' $7 billion plan to remake Houston highways once again targets homes, businesses in communities of color." *The Texas Tribune.* https://www.texastribune.org/2019/10/11/texas-plan-remake-houston-highways-targets-communities-color/

[19]AAA. 2017. "Your Driving Costs." AAA Newsroom. https://newsroom.aaa.com/auto/your-driving-costs/

[20]"Road Traffic Injuries." 2018. World Health Organization https://www.who.int/en/news-room/fact-sheets/detail/road-traffic-injuries

[21]Halsey III, Ashley. 2019. "More Americans have died in car crashes since 2000 than in both World Wars." *The Washington Post.* https://www.washingtonpost.com/local/trafficandcommuting/more-people-died-in-car-crashes-this-century-than-in-both-world-wars/2019/07/21/0ecc0006-3f54-11e9-9361-301ffb5bd5e6_story.html

[22]"Global status report on road safety 2018: Summary" 2018. World Health Organization. https://apps.who.int/iris/bitstream/handle/10665/277370/WHO-NMH-NVI-18.20-eng.pdf?ua=1

[23]Richards, James. 2014. "Sweden's Vision Zero to Eliminate Traffic Fatalities." Slater Vecchio, LLP. https://www.slatervecchio.com/swedens-vision-zero-to-eliminate-traffic-fatalities/

[24]"Vision Zero: Mayor de Blasio Announces That Traffic Fatalities are Expected to Drop for Fifth Straight Year." 2018. City of New York. https://www1.nyc.gov/office-of-the-mayor/news/621-18/vision-zero-mayor-de-blasio-that-traffic-fatalities-expected-drop-fifth

[25]Trufant, Anthony L. 2017. "Zero for Vision Zero." Patch. https://patch.com/new-york/fortgreene/zero-vision-zero

[26]Stein, Perry. 2015. "Can some big D.C. churches fight off a bike lane? They are bringing large crowds to try." *The Washington Post.* https://www.washingtonpost.com/news/local/wp/2015/10/23/can-some-big-d-c-churches-fight-off-a-bike-lane-they-are-bringing-large-crowds-to-try/

Chapter 4

[1]Keane, Sean. 2019. "Tim Cook reminds us about Apple's sustainability efforts." Cnet. https://www.cnet.com/news/tim-cook-reminds-us-about-apples-sustainability-efforts/

[2]"The Cornwall Declaration on Environmental Stewardship." 2010. Cornwall Alliance for the Stewardship of Creation. https://cornwallalliance.org/landmark-documents/the-cornwall-declaration-on-environmental-stewardship/

[3]"Full text of SBECI declaration." 2008. Baptist Press. http://www.bpnews.net/27585/full-text-of-sbeci-declaration

[4]"NASA, NOAA Data Show 2016 Warmest Year on Record Globally." 2017. National Aeronautics and Space Administration, Goddard Institute for Space Studies. https://www.giss.nasa.gov/research/news/20170118/

[5]Borunda, Alejandra. 2019. "The last five years were the hottest ever recorded." *National Geographic*. https://www.nationalgeographic.com/environment/2019/02/2018-fourth-warmest-year-ever-noaa-nasa-reports/

[6]"Scientific Consensus: Earth's Climate is Warming." 2020. NASA Global Climate Change. https://climate.nasa.gov/scientific-consensus/

[7]Lindsey, Rebecca. 2019. "Climate Change: Global Sea Level." National Oceanic and Atmospheric Administration. https://www.climate.gov/news-features/understanding-climate/climate-change-global-sea-level

[8]Morrison, Jim. 2018. "Flooding Hot Spots: Why Seas Are Rising Faster on the U.S. East Coast." *Yale Environment 360*, Yale School of Forestry & Environmental Studies. https://e360.yale.edu/features/flooding-hot-spots-why-seas-are-rising-faster-on-the-u.s.-cast-coast

[9]Holder, Josh, Kommenda, Niko and Watts, Jonathan. 2017. "The three-degree world: the cities that will be drowned by global warming." The Guardian. https://www.theguardian.com/cities/ng-interactive/2017/nov/03/three-degree-world-cities-drowned-global-warming

[10]Biography of Katharine Hayhoe found at http://katharinehayhoe.com/wp2016/biography/

[11]"Hot Science, Cool Talks: Climate and Faith, Money and Politics Featuring Katharine Hayhoe." 2017. Live event, Paramount Theatre, Austin, Texas.

[12]Graham, Steve. 1999. "John Tyndall (1820-1893)." Earth Observatory. NASA. https://earthobservatory.nasa.gov/features/Tyndall

[13]Merritt, Jonathan. 2010. *Green Like God: Unlocking the Divine Plan for Our Planet.*

14"Asthma: Key Facts" 2017. World Health Organization. https://www.who.int/news-room/fact-sheets/detail/asthma

15Akinbami, MD, Lara J., et. al. 2009. "Status of Childhood Asthma in the United States, 1980-2007. *Pediatrics*. 123 (3).

16"Most Recent National Asthma Data." 2017. Centers for Disease Control and Prevention. https://www.cdc.gov/asthma/most_recent_national_asthma_data.htm

17Yeomans, Ph.D., Tim. 2018. "Does Being Too Clean Cause Allergies?" Allergy Standards. https://www.allergystandards.com/news_events/hygiene-hypothesis/

18"Sources of Greenhouse Gas Emissions." 2019. United States Environmental Protection Agency. https://www.epa.gov/ghgemissions/sources-greenhouse-gas-emissions

19Adar, D'Souza, Sheppard, et al. 2015. "Adopting Clean Fuels and Technologies on School Buses: Pollution and Health Impacts in Children." *American Journal of Respiratory and Critical Care Medicine*. 191 (12), 1413-1421.

20Lee, B. J., Kim, B., & Lee, K. 2014. "Air pollution exposure and cardiovascular disease." *Toxicological research*, 30(2), 71–75.

21"Transportation Health Impact Assessment Toolkit." 2011. Centers for Disease Control and Prevention. https://www.cdc.gov/healthyplaces/transportation/hia_toolkit.htm

22"AAA Gas Prices" 2020. https://gasprices.aaa.com/

23Calculated by dividing the average number of miles driven annually by the average fuel efficiency of new vehicles, multiplied by the average price per gallon for gasoline. Sources:
"Average Annual Miles per Driver by Age Group" 2018. U.S. Department of Transportation Federal Highway Administration. https://www.fhwa.dot.gov/ohim/onh00/bar8.htm
Shepardson, David. 2019. "U.S. auto fleet hit record high fuel efficiency in 2017." Reuters. https://www.reuters.com/article/us-epa-emissions-autos/u-s-auto-fleet-hit-record-high-fuel-efficiency-in-2017-idUSKCN1QN23N

24Probert, Andy. 2018. "Solar Energy Grows More Affordable as Panel Prices Fall Faster Than Experts Predicted." Greener Ideal. https://greenerideal.com/news/solar-panel-prices-fall-faster-than-experts-predict/

25"Solar Industry Research Data" 2019. Solar Energy Industries Association. https://www.seia.org/solar-industry-research-data

[26]Aggarwal, Vikram. 2019. "How to calculate solar panel payback period (ROI)." EnergySage. https://news.energysage.com/understanding-your-solar-panel-payback-period/

[27]Sanchez, Valentina. 2019. "Solar power can boost your home's value--especially in these 10 states." CNBC. https://www.cnbc.com/2019/10/05/solar-power-can-boost-a-homes-value-in-these-10-states-the-most.html

[28]Scott, Mike. 2019. "Battery Factories Power Up to Cut Costs and Drive Electric Car Revolution." *Forbes*. https://www.forbes.com/sites/mikescott/2019/12/13/battery-production-powers-up-as-costs-head-towards-100kwh/#64b46bf43466

[29]"Kona Electric." 2020. Hyundai Motor America. https://www.hyundaiusa.com/kona-electric/index.aspx

[30]"The Longest-Range Electric Vehicle Now Goes Even Farther." 2019. Tesla. https://www.tesla.com/blog/longest-range-electric-vehicle-now-goes-even-farther

[31]"DART Fares." 2020. Dallas Area Rapid Transit. https://www.dart.org/fares/fares.asp

[32]"TriMet Fares." 2020. TriMet. https://trimet.org/fares/index.htm#adult

[33]"Auto-pay Monthly Passes." 2020. Massachusetts Bay Transportation Authority. https://www.mbta.com/fares/auto-pay

[34]Hirtenstein, Anna. 2016. "Clean-Energy Jobs Surpass Oil Drilling for First Time in U.S." *Bloomberg*. https://www.bloomberg.com/news/articles/2016-05-25/clean-energy-jobs-surpass-oil-drilling-for-first-time-in-u-s

[35]Marcacci, Silvio. 2019. "Renewable Energy Job Boom Creates Economic Opportunity As Coal Industry Slumps." *Forbes*. https://www.forbes.com/sites/energyinnovation/2019/04/22/renewable-energy-job-boom-creating-economic-opportunity-as-coal-industry-slumps/#719afda33665

[36]"Employment in Renewable Energy Sector Reaches 5.7 Million Globally." 2014. International Renewable Energy Agency. https://www.irena.org/newsroom/pressreleases/2014/Jan/Employment-in-Renewable-Energy-Sector-Reaches-57-Million-Globally

[37]"11 Million People Employed in Renewable Energy Worldwide in 2018." 2019. International Renewable Energy Agency. https://www.irena.org/newsroom/pressreleases/2019/Jun/11-Million-People-Employed-in-Renewable-Energy-Worldwide-in-2018

[38]Flinker, Peter. 2010. "The Need to Reduce Impervious Cover to Prevent Flooding and Protect Water Quality." Rhode Island Department of Environmental Management. http://www.dem.ri.gov/programs/bpoladm/suswshed/pdfs/imperv.pdf

[39]Dance, Scott. 2019. "Baltimore, Annapolis set records for sunny-day flooding in 2018--and it could eventually occur every other day." *The Baltimore Sun*. https://www.baltimoresun.com/weather/bs-md-nuisance-flooding-record-20190710-c6kx6hnih-jgubkhkqq5qnl5vuy-story.html

[40]"FEMA Fact Sheet: Mitigation Assessment Team Results - Hurricane Sandy." 2018. Department of Homeland Security. https://www.fema.gov/mat-results-hurricane-sandy

[41]Florido, Adrian. 2018. "Puerto Rico Estimates it Will Cost $139 Billion to Fully Recover from Hurricane Maria." NPR. https://www.npr.org/2018/08/09/637230089/puerto-rico-estimates-it-will-cost-139-billion-to-fully-recover-from-hurricane-m

[42]"Drought: Monitoring Economic, Environmental, and Social Impacts." NOAA National Centers for Environmental Information. https://www.ncdc.noaa.gov/news/drought-monitoring-economic-environmental-and-social-impacts

[43]See 13.

[44]"Responsible Forestry." 2020. World Wildlife Fund. https://www.worldwildlife.org/industries/responsible-forestry

[45]"Deforestation and Forest Degradation." 2020. World Wildlife Fund. https://www.worldwildlife.org/threats/deforestation-and-forest-degradation

[46]"Climate Impacts on Agriculture and Food Supply." 2017. United States Environmental Protection Agency. https://archive.epa.gov/epa/climate-impacts/climate-impacts-agriculture-and-food-supply.html

[47]Myers, Samuel S. et al. 2014. "Rising CO_2 threatens human nutrition." *Nature*, 510(7504), 139-142.

[48]Olson, Carolyn. 2018. "Chapter 10: Agriculture and Rural Communities." Fourth National Climate Assessment, U.S. Global Change Research Program. https://nca2018.globalchange.gov/chapter/10/

[49]Lesk, C., Rowhani, P. & Ramankutty, N. 2016. "Influence of extreme weather disasters on global crop production." *Nature*, 529, 84-87.

[50]"World deforestation slows down as more forests are better managed." 2015. Food and Agriculture Organization of the United Nations. http://www.fao.org/news/story/en/item/326911/icode/

[51]"New record: Number of overfished stocks in the U.S. reaches all time low." 2018. National Oceanic and Atmospheric Administration. https://www.noaa.gov/media-release/new-record-number-of-overfished-stocks-in-us-reaches-all-time-low

[52]"Tackling overfishing—EU push for sustainability shows results." 2018. European Commission. https://ec.europa.eu/fisheries/tackling-overfishing-%E2%80%93-eu-push-sustainability-shows-results_en

[53]Shapiro, Joseph S. & Walker, Reed. 2015. "Why is pollution from U.S. manufacturing declining? The roles of trade, regulation, productivity, and preferences." Cowles Foundation for Research in Economics, Yale University. https://cowles.yale.edu/sites/default/files/files/pub/d19/d1982.pdf

[54]"Mars Inc. achieves zero waste to landfill." 2016. *Recycling Today.* https://www.recyclingtoday.com/article/mars-reaches-zero-waste-to-landfill-goal/

[55]Hendricks, David. 2016. "Look, in the sky, it's lower emissions." *San Antonio Express-News.* https://www.expressnews.com/business/business_columnists/david_hendricks/article/Look-in-the-sky-it-s-lower-emissions-6746540.php

[56]"Solar Innovators." Azuri Technologies. https://www.azuri-group.com/about/

[57]"About us." 2020. Fairphone. https://www.fairphone.com/en/about/about-us/

[58]"About Greenscape." 2013. Greenscape Eco Management. http://greenscape-eco.com/company/about-us/

[59]Ritchie, Hannah. 2020. "You want to reduce the carbon footprint of your food? Focus on what you eat, not whether your food is local." Our World in Data. https://ourworldindata.org/food-choice-vs-eating-local

[60]Thompson, Helen. 2015. "The Case for Washing Clothes in Cold Water." *Smithsonian Magazine.* https://www.smithsonianmag.com/smart-news/case-washing-clothes-cold-water-180955459/

[61]See 11.

Chapter 5

[1]"Dura-Europos House Church." 2019. Wondermondo. https://www.wondermondo.com/dura-europos-house-church/

[2]Keys, David. 1998. "Earliest church discovered in Red Sea port." *The Independent.* https://www.independent.co.uk/news/earliest-church-discovered-in-red-sea-port-1193713.html

[3]"St. Peter's Basilica." Wikipedia. https://en.wikipedia.org/wiki/St._Peter%27s_Basilica

[4]"How big is the White House?" The White House Historical Association. https://www.whitehousehistory.org/questions/how-big-is-the-white-house

184 Faith in Cities

[5]"Lakewood Church Central Campus." 2020. Fandom. https://houstonrockets. fandom.com/wiki/Lakewood_Church_Central_Campus

[6]Zaimov, Stoyan. 2016. "Joel Osteen's Lakewood Church Ranked America's Largest Megachurch With 52,000 Weekly Attendance." *The Christian Post.* https://www. christianpost.com/news/joel-osteens-lakewood-church-ranked-americas-largest-megachurch-with-52k-in-attendance-169279

[7]"Database of Megachurches in the U.S." 2015. Hartford Institute for Religion Research. http://hirr.hartsem.edu/megachurch/database.html

[8]"Largest Churches in America." 2019. Outreach 100. https://outreach100.com/ largest-churches-in-america

[9]Community Bible Church. https://www.communitybible.com/

[10]Silverberg, Melissa. 2014. "Arlington Heights, church settle parking dispute." *Daily Herald.* https://www.dailyherald.com/article/20140805/news/140809372/

[11]Lantrip, Patrick. 2016. "York Avenue Residents to Protest IC Expansion." *Memphis Daily News.* https://www.memphisdailynews.com/news/2016/nov/16/york-avenue-residents-to-protest-ic-expansion//print

[12]Liberatore, Wendy. 2016. "Clifton Park residents oppose expanded Northway Church near Northway exit." *Albany Times Union.* https://www.mrt.com/local/article/Clifton-Park-residents-oppose-expanded-Northway-9371805.php

[13]Smith, J.B. 2011. "Faith-motivated newcomers take root in North Waco." *Waco Tribune-Herald.* https://www.wacotrib.com/news/faith-motivated-newcomers-take-root-in-north-waco/article_28d8b1d1-02a8-5e3c-b9b5-ccd88e0e5929.html

[14]Bilezikian, Gilbert. 2009. *Community 101.*

[15]Wilford, Justin. 2012. *Sacred Subdivisions: The Postsuburban Transformation of American Evangelicalism.* NYU Press.

[16]Eastman, Brett. 2008. "The Power and Potential of Small Groups." *Enrichment,* 13(1).

[17]Busby, Matt. 2016. "Three Practices for Third Space Churches." *Christianity Today.* https://www.christianitytoday.com/edstetzer/2016/september/three-practices-for-third-space-churches.html

[18]Third Church RVA. https://www.thirdrva.org/

Chapter 6

[1]Wilson, Kirby. 2017. "Anti-cyberbullying activists wanted a Texas law with 'teeth.' They may have gotten one." *The Texas Tribune.* https://www.texastribune. org/2017/09/14/anti-cyberbullying-activists-wanted-law-has-teeth-they-may-have-gotten/

[2]Earl, Jennifer. 2016. "Texas man posts message to cyber bullies after teen brother's suicide." CBS News. https://www.cbsnews.com/news/mans-message-to-bullies-after-teen-brothers-suicide-goes-viral/

[3]Moredock, Will. 2014. "Ben Tillman was a racist, terrorist, and murderer: It's time to take down his statue." *Charleston City Paper.* https://www.charlestoncitypaper.com/charleston/ben-tillman-was-a-racist-terrorist-and-murderer-its-time-to-take-down-his-statue/Content?oid=4857402

[4]Berman, Mark. 2015. "Even more black people were lynched in the U.S. than previously thought, study finds." *The Washington Post.* https://www.washingtonpost.com/news/post-nation/wp/2015/02/10/even-more-black-people-were-lynched-in-the-u-s-than-previously-thought-study-finds/

[5]"Delaware Ratifies Thirteenth Amendment 36 Years Later." Equal Justice Initiative. https://calendar.eji.org/racial-injustice/feb/12

[6]"2017 Hate Crime Statistics, Table 1." Federal Bureau of Investigation. https://ucr. fbi.gov/hate-crime/2017/tables/table-1.xls

[7]"Race-Based Charges (Charges filed with EEOC) FY 1997 - FY 2019." U.S. Equal Employment Opportunity Commission. https://www.eeoc.gov/eeoc/statistics/enforcement/race.cfm

[8]"Defending Against Unprecedented Attacks on Fair Housing: 2019 Fair Housing Trends Report." 2019. National Fair Housing Alliance. https://nationalfairhousing. org/wp-content/uploads/2019/10/2019-Trends-Report.pdf

[9]Tenger, Tisa. 2017. "Discriminating in the name of religion? Segregationists and slaveholders did it, too." *The Washington Post.* https://www.washingtonpost.com/news/made-by-history/wp/2017/12/05/discriminating-in-the-name-of-religion-segregationists-and-slaveholders-did-it-too/

[10]Robert P. Jones, Natalie Jackson, Maxine Najle, Oyindamola Bola, and Daniel Greenberg. 2019. "Increasing Support for Religiously Based Service Refusals." *PRRI.* https://www.prri.org/research/increasing-support-for-religiously-based-service-refusals/.

[11]Jones, Robert P., and Cox, Daniel. 2015. "Deep Divide Between Black and White Americans in Views of Criminal Justice System." *PRRI.* https://www.prri.org/research/divide-white-black-americans-criminal-justice-system/

[12]Wright, Bradley R. E., et al. 2015. "Religion, Race, and Discrimination: A Field Experiment of How American Churches Welcome Newcomers." *Journal for the Scientific Study of Religion*, 54(2).

[13]Carpenter, Vincent. 2017. "The Culture of Heaven: A Biblical Perspective on Diversity, Part 2." Antioch Community Church, Waco, Texas (Sermon).

[14]Williams, Rhys, Emerson, Michael, & Smith, Christian. 2004. "Divided by Faith: Evangelical Religion and the Problem of Race in America. *Sociology of Religion*, 65(2).

[15]Dwyer-Lindgren L, Bertozzi-Villa A, Stubbs RW, et al. 2014. "Inequalities in Life Expectancy Among US Counties, 1980 to 2014: Temporal Trends and Key Drivers." *JAMA Intern Medicine* 177 (7): 1003–1011. https://doi.org/10.1001/jamainternmed.2017.0918

[16]Jesdale, Bill M., Morello-Frosch, Rachel, and Cushing, Lara. 2013. "The Racial/Ethnic Distribution of Heat Risk–Related Land Cover in Relation to Residential Segregation." *Environmental Health Perspectives*, 121: 811-817. http://dx.doi.org/10.1289/ehp.1205919

[17]Stromberg, Joseph. 2015. "The forgotten history of how automakers invented the crime of 'jaywalking'." *Vox*. https://www.vox.com/2015/1/15/7551873/jaywalking-history

[18]Marshall, Colin. 2016. "Story of cities #29: Los Angeles and the 'great American streetcar scandal'." *The Guardian*. https://www.theguardian.com/cities/2016/apr/25/story-cities-los-angeles-great-american-streetcar-scandal

[19]National Highway Traffic Safety Administration. Motor Vehicle Traffic Fatalities and Fatality Rates, 1899-2017. https://cdan.nhtsa.gov/tsftables/Fatalities%20and%20Fatality%20Rates.pdf

[20]Smart Growth America. Dangerous by Design 2016. http://s3.amazonaws.com/cdn.smartgrowthamerica.org/dangerous-by-design-2016.pdf

[21]Lopez, R.P. and Hynes, H.P. 2006. "Obesity, physical activity, and the urban environment: public health research needs." *Environmental Health* 5, (25) doi:10.1186/1476-069X-5-25

[22]Marshall, Wesley E. and Garrick, Norman W. 2011. "Does street network design affect traffic safety?" *Accident Analysis & Prevention* 43, (3): 769-781. https://doi.org/10.1016/j.aap.2010.10.024

[23]HSH Associates. The salary you must earn to buy a home in the 50 largest metros. https://www.hsh.com/finance/mortgage/salary-home-buying-25-cities.html

[24]Tekin, Eylul. "A Timeline of Affordability: How Have Home Prices and Household Incomes Changed Since 1960?" Clever. https://listwithclever.com/real-estate-blog/home-price-v-income-historical-study/

[25]Canada Mortgage and Housing Corporation. 2018. Examining Escalating House Prices in Large Canadian Metropolitan Centres. CMHC. https://www.straight.com/files/v3/files/cmhc_housing_study.pdf

[26]Bengtsson, Helena and Lyons, Kate. 2015. "Revealed: the widening gulf between salaries and house prices." *The Guardian.* https://www.theguardian.com/uk-news/2015/sep/02/housing-market-gulf-salaries-house-prices

[27]Glaeser, Edward, and Joseph Gyourko. 2018. "The Economic Implications of Housing Supply." *Journal of Economic Perspectives*, 32, (1): 3-30.

[28]Desmond, Matthew. 2017. *Evicted: Poverty and Profit in the American City.*

[29]Stellar, J.E., Manzo, V.M., Kraus, M.W., and Keltner, D. 2012. "Class and compassion: socioeconomic factors predict responses to suffering." *Emotion.* 12 (3): 449-59. doi: 10.1037/a0026508.

[30]Grewal, Daisy. 2012. "How wealth reduces compassion." *Scientific American.* https://www.scientificamerican.com/article/how-wealth-reduces-compassion/

[31]Roberts, David. 2015. "How our housing choices make adult friendships more difficult." *Vox.* https://www.vox.com/2015/10/28/9622920/housing-adult-friendship

[32]Metzger, Paul Louis. 2010. "What is Biblical Justice?" *Christianity Today.* https://www.christianitytoday.com/pastors/2010/summer/biblicaljustice.html

[33]Wallis, Jim. 2014. *The (Un)Common Good: How the Gospel Brings Hope to a World Divided.*

[34]Evans, Tony. 2015. *Oneness Embraced: Reconciliation, the Kingdom, and How we are Stronger Together.*

[35]ten Boom, Corrie. 2014. "Guideposts Classics: Corrie ten Boom on Forgiveness." Guideposts. https://www.guideposts.org/better-living/positive-living/guideposts-classics-corrie-ten-boom-on-forgiveness

[36]Keller, Timothy. 2012. *Generous Justice: How God's Grace Makes Us Just.*

[37]National Alliance to End Homelessness. 2019. State of Homelessness. https://endhomelessness.org/homelessness-in-america/homelessness-statistics/state-of-homelessness-report/

[38]Joint Center for Housing Studies of Harvard University. 2017. Renter Cost Burdens, States. https://www.jchs.harvard.edu/ARH_2017_cost_burdens_by_state_total

[39]United Nations High Commissioner for Refugees. 2019. Figures at a Glance: Statistical Yearbooks. https://www.unhcr.org/en-us/figures-at-a-glance.html

[40]Lupton, Robert D. 2007. *Compassion, Justice, and the Christian Life: Rethinking Ministry to the Poor.*

[41]Piper, John. 2015. "Biblical Foundations for Seeking God's Justice in a Sinful World." Video from a panel discussion at The Gospel Coalition's 2015 National Conference, Coming Home: New Heaven and New Earth. https://www.thegospel-coalition.org/conference/2015-national-conference/

[42]Wytsma, Ken. 2017. *The Myth of Equality: Uncovering the Roots of Injustice and Privilege.*

Chapter 7

[1]"The Population of Poverty USA." 2020. Poverty USA. https://www.povertyusa.org/facts

[2]"The 20 countries with the largest gross domestic product (GDP) per capita in 2019." 2019. Statista. https://www.statista.com/statistics/270180/countries-with-the-largest-gross-domestic-product-gdp-per-capita/

[3]Kroll, Luisa & Dolan. Kerry A. 2019. "Billionaires: The Richest People in the World." *Forbes.* https://www.forbes.com/billionaires/#69c9fb9a251c

[4]Bowden, Ebony. 2019. "The US has more millionaires than Greece has people." *New York Post.* https://nypost.com/2019/03/14/the-us-has-more-millionaires-than-greece-has-people/

[5]"Hair & Nail Salons in the US Market Size 2000-2025." 2020. IBISWorld. https://www.ibisworld.com/industry-statistics/market-size/hair-nail-salons-united-states/

[6]"GDP Ranked by Country 2020." 2020. World Population Review. http://world-populationreview.com/countries/countries-by-gdp/

[7]"Pet Industry Market Size & Ownership Statistics." 2020. American Pet Products Association. https://www.americanpetproducts.org/press_industrytrends.asp

[8]"Restaurant Industry Facts at a Glance." 2020. National Restaurant Association. https://www.restaurant.org/research/restaurant-statistics/restaurant-industry-facts-at-a-glance

[9]Perez, Sarah. 2019. "Paid streaming music subscriptions in US top 60M, says RIAA." *TechCrunch*. https://techcrunch.com/2019/09/06/paid-streaming-music-subscriptions-in-u-s-top-60m-says-riaa/

[10]Feiner, Lauren. 2019. "Hulu gained twice as many US subscribers as Netflix at the start of 2019." *CNBC*. https://www.cnbc.com/2019/05/01/hulu-gained-twice-as-many-subscribers-as-netflix-in-us.html
Note: according to the U.S. Census Bureau there are 119.7 million households in the United States, which suggests at least half of all households pay for either Hulu or Netflix, or both.

[11]"Media Center." 2020. International Health, Racquet & Sportsclub Association. https://www.ihrsa.org/about/media-center/

[12]"Revenue of the apparel market worldwide by country in 2018." 2019. Statista. https://www.statista.com/forecasts/758683/revenue-of-the-apparel-market-worldwide-by-country

[13]"Average New-Vehicle Prices Up 3.5% Year-Over-Year in January 2020 on Sales Mix, According to Kelley Blue Book." 2020. Kelley Blue Book. https://mediaroom.kbb.com/2020-02-18-Average-New-Vehicle-Prices-Up-3-5-Year-Over-Year-in-January-2020-on-Sales-Mix-According-to-Kelley-Blue-Book

[14]Capparella, Joey. 2020. "25 Best-Selling Cars, Trucks, and SUVs of 2019." *Car and Driver*. https://www.caranddriver.com/news/g27041933/best-selling-cars-2019/

[15]Atiyeh, Clifford. 2019. "Americans Are Taking Out Ridiculously Long Auto Loans." *Car and Driver*. https://www.caranddriver.com/news/a29338445/auto-loans-expensive-longer/

[16]"New and Existing Home Sales, U.S." 2020. National Association of Home Builders. https://www.nahb.org/-/media/NAHB/news-and-economics/docs/economics/Sales/nationwide-home-sales-and-inventory-december-2019.pdf

[17]White, Marian. 2019. "US Moving Statistics for 2019." Moving.com https://www.moving.com/tips/us-moving-statistics-for-2019/

[18]Harris, Alexander. 2019. "U.S. self-storage industry statistics." SpareFoot Storage Beat. https://www.sparefoot.com/self-storage/news/1432-self-storage-industry-statistics/

[19]XSpace. https://xspacegroup.com/

[20]McGinn, Daniel. 2008. *House Lust: America's Obsession With Our Homes*.

[21]The average cost per square foot to build a new home is about $150, nationally. Source: HomeAdvisor https://www.homeadvisor.com/cost/architects-and-engineers/build-a-house/

[22]Arnold, Jeanne E., Graesch, Anthony P., Ragazzini, Enzo, and Ochs, Elinor. 2012. *Life at Home in the Twenty-First Century: 32 Families Open Their Doors.*

[23]"Frequently Asked Questions." LifeEdited. https://lifeedited.com/frequently-asked-questions/

[24]"Global advertising spending from 2010 to 2019." 2018. Statista. https://www.statista.com/statistics/236943/global-advertising-spending/

[25]Fernandez, Chantal. 2015. "Fashion Magazines Stay Mum on September Ad Page Numbers." Fashionista. https://fashionista.com/2015/08/september-ad-pages-hand-count

[26]Myers, David G. 2001. *The American Paradox: Spiritual Hunger in an Age of Plenty.*

[27]Cortright, Joe. 2019. "There is Nothing Super About 'Super-Commuting." Strong Towns. https://www.strongtowns.org/journal/2019/9/24/there-is-nothing-super-about-supercommuting

[28]Haden, Jeff. 2016. "Want to Stay Married? Science Says Reconsider a Long Commute (Since the Money Isn't Worth It)." *Inc.* https://www.inc.com/jeff-haden/want-to-stay-married-science-says-reconsider-a-long-commute-since-the-money-isnt.html

[29]Roberts, David. 2017. "Young families typically leave cities for the suburbs. Here's how to keep them downtown." *Vox.* https://www.vox.com/2017/6/21/15815524/toderian-families-cities

[30]City of Vancouver. 2016. "Family Room: Housing Mix Policy for Rezoning Projects." https://council.vancouver.ca/20160713/documents/cfsc2.pdf

[31]"Downtown Demographics." 2019. Downtown Seattle Association. https://downtownseattle.org/programs-and-services/research-and-development/residents/

[32]Scholes, Jon and George, Emily. 2017. "Seattle families need a new downtown high school." *The Seattle Times.* https://www.seattletimes.com/opinion/seattle-families-need-a-new-downtown-high-school/

[33]Garland, Anthony Charles. 2007. *A Testimony of Jesus Christ, Volume 1: A Commentary on the Book of Revelation.*

[34]Biediger, Shari. 2017. "Panic at the Pump: Gas Shortages and Rising Prices Fuel Long Lines." *The Rivard Report.* https://therivardreport.com/panic-at-the-pump-gas-shortages-and-rising-prices-fuel-long-lines/

[35]Robinson, Elizabeth. 2017. "VIA providing free bus rides Sept. 5 in response San Antonio gas shortage." *San Antonio Express-News.* https://www.mysanantonio.com/news/local/traffic/article/VIA-providing-free-bus-rides-Sept-5-in-response-12172436.php

[36]"Consumer Expenditures--2018." 2019. U.S. Bureau of Labor Statistics. https://www.bls.gov/news.release/cesan.nr0.htm

[37]El Issa, Erin. 2019. "2019 American Household Credit Card Debt Study." Nerd-Wallet. https://www.nerdwallet.com/blog/average-credit-card-debt-household/

[38]Picchi, Aimee. 2019. "70% of Americans say they are struggling financially." *CBS News*. https://www.cbsnews.com/news/70-americans-are-struggling-financially/

[39]Sheridan, Kate. 2017. "Rich countries are more anxious than poorer countries. *Stat*. https://www.statnews.com/2017/03/15/anxiety-rich-country-poor-country/

[40]Shinabarger, Jeff. 2013. *More or Less: Choosing a Lifestyle of Excessive Generosity*.

[41]Beyer, Scott. 2016. "Miami's Parking Deregulation Will Reduce Housing Costs." *Forbes*. https://www.forbes.com/sites/scottbeyer/2016/07/15/miamis-parking-deregulation-will-reduce-housing-costs/#b2407bb2ca6d

[42]Curry, Melanie. 2015. "Governor Signs Bill to Ease Parking Requirements for Affordable Housing." Streetsblog. https://cal.streetsblog.org/2015/10/12/governor-brown-signs-bill-loosening-parking-requirements-for-affordable-housing/

Chapter 8

[1]AmeriCorps VISTA Fact Sheet 2017. https://www.nationalservice.gov/sites/default/files/documents/AmeriCorps-VISTA-Fact-Sheet-2017_1.pdf

[2]Fessler, Pam. 2015. "Why Disability and Poverty Still Go Hand In Hand 25 Years After Landmark Law." *National Public Radio*. https://www.npr.org/sections/health-shots/2015/07/23/424990474/why-disability-and-poverty-still-go-hand-in-hand-25-years-after-landmark-law

[3]Fact Sheet: Social Security. 2019. Social Security Administration. https://www.ssa.gov/news/press/factsheets/colafacts2019.pdf

[4]Stallen, Mirre. 2017. "Poverty and the Developing Brain." Behavioral Scientist. https://behavioralscientist.org/can-neuroscientists-help-us-understand-fight-effects-childhood-poverty/

[5]"Childhood Lead Poisoning Prevention: At-Risk Populations." 2019. Centers for Disease Control and Prevention. https://www.cdc.gov/nceh/lead/prevention/populations.htm

[6]Katz, Cheryl. 2012. "People in Poor Neighborhoods Breathe More Hazardous Particles." *Scientific American*. https://www.scientificamerican.com/article/people-poor-neighborhoods-breate-more-hazardous-particles/

[7]Kravitz-Wirtz, Nicole, et al. 2018. Early-Life Air Pollution Exposure, Neighborhood Poverty, and Childhood Asthma in the United States, 1990-2014. *International Journal of Environmental Research and Public Health*, 15(6). doi: 10.3390/ijerph15061114

[8]Seaton, Jaimie. 2017. "Reading, writing and hunger: More than 13 million kids in this country go to school hungry." *The Washington Post*. https://www.washingtonpost. com/news/parenting/wp/2017/03/09/reading-writing-and-hunger-more-than-13-million-kids-in-this-country-go-to-school-hungry/

[9]Hodgkinson, S., Godoy, L., Beers, L. S., & Lewin, A. 2017. Improving Mental Health Access for Low-Income Children and Families in the Primary Care Setting. *Pediatrics*, 139(1). https://doi.org/10.1542/peds.2015-1175

[10]"Children Who Repeated a Grade." 2018. Child Trends. https://www.childtrends. org/indicators/children-who-repeated-a-grade-2

[11]Livingston, Gretchen. 2018. "The Changing Profile of Unmarried Parents." Pew Research Center. https://www.pewsocialtrends.org/2018/04/25/the-changing-profile-of-unmarried-parents/

[12]Cain Miller, Claire and Tedeschi, Ernie. 2019. "Single Mothers Are Surging Into the Work Force." *The New York Times*. https://www.nytimes.com/2019/05/29/upshot/single-mothers-surge-employment.html

[13]Chan, Sewin and Khun Jush, Gita. "2017 National Rental Housing Landscape: Renting in the Nation's Largest Metros." NYU Furman Center. https://furman-center.org/files/NYUFurmanCenter_2017_National_Rental_Housing_Landscape_04OCT2017.pdf

[14]Lynch, Matthew. 2014. "High School Dropout Rate: Causes and Costs." *The Huffington Post*. https://www.huffpost.com/entry/high-school-dropout-rate_b_5421778?guccounter=1&guce_referrer=aHR0cHM6Ly93d3cuZ29vZ2xlLmNvbS88&guce_referrer_sig=AQAAAGuAEVZ4aHjRd2laM2UX-3PVoVocdDTt4R05CpJPb3S2goibGq9iUi56FuUBxvvjfDvXbxkd7BZw3_hsUKLgzrAbOzhUuwDE3jGufVpqFxFl9H9r0bUdPFk4sHLhF5gHzEZjRd-wiNkAz3ojiM76KSyXyfIkgyQvTkDc_3d34ScTee

[15]Feeney, Lauren. 2016. "Why the Poor Pay More." Chasing the Dream: Poverty & Opportunity in America, *PBS*. https://www.pbs.org/wnet/chasing-the-dream/stories/why-the-poor-pay-more/

[16]Ellen, Barbara. 2017. "The warped logic of making the poor pay more." *The Guardian*. https://www.theguardian.com/commentisfree/2017/oct/15/the-warped-logic-of-making-the-poor-pay-more

[17]Chetty, R., Hendren, N., Kline, P. & Saez, E. 2014. Where is the Land of Opportunity? The Geography of Intergenerational Mobility in the United States. Harvard University and National Bureau of Economic Research. https://scholar.harvard. edu/files/hendren/files/nbhds_paper.pdf

[18]Kaufman, S.M., Moss, M.L., Hernandez, J. & Tyndall, J. 2015. Mobiliti, Economic Opportunity and New York City Neighborhoods. The Rudin Center for Transportation at New York University. https://wagner.nyu.edu/files/faculty/publications/ JobAccessNov2015.pdf

[19]Jordan, Mary & Sullivan, Kevin. 2017. "The new reality of old age in America." *The Washington Post.* https://www.washingtonpost.com/graphics/2017/national/ seniors-financial-insecurity/

[20]Berg, Austin. 2015. "Illinois' Warped Welfare System Traps Families in Poverty." Illinois Policy Institute. https://www.illinoispolicy.org/illinois-warped-welfare-sys-tem-traps-families-in-poverty/

[21]Tanner, Michael & Hughes, Charles. 2013. "The Work Versus Welfare Trade-Off: 2013." The Cato Institute. https://www.cato.org/sites/cato.org/files/pubs/pdf/ the_work_versus_welfare_trade-off_2013_wp.pdf

[22]"The Long Wait for a Home." 2016. National Low Income Housing Coalition. https://nlihc.org/sites/default/files/HousingSpotlight_6-1.pdf

[23]Banerjee, A.V., Hanna, R., Kreindler, G.E., & Olken, B.A. 2017. Debunking the Stereotype of the Lazy Welfare Recipient: Evidence from Cash Transfer Programs. *The World Bank Research Observer*, 32 (2). https://doi.org/10.1093/wbro/lkx002

[24]"Who Said That?" 2014. *Governing.* https://www.governing.com/govern-ment-quotes/gov-we-dont-want-to-turn-the-safety-net-into-a-hammock-that-lulls-able-bodied-people-to-lives-of-dependency-and-complacency.html

[25]Aziz, John. 2014. "Does welfare make people lazy?" *The Week.* https://theweek. com/articles/449215/does-welfare-make-people-lazy

[26]"Higher wage workers more likely than lower wage workers to have paid leave benefits in 2018." 2018. Bureau of Labor Statistics. https://www.bls.gov/opub/ ted/2018/higher-wage-workers-more-likely-than-lower-wage-workers-to-have-paid-leave-benefits-in-2018.htm

[27]Ballman, Donna. 2013. "Can You Be Fired for Calling In Sick--Even With A Doctor's Note?" Aol. https://www.aol.com/2013/03/14/fired-missing-work-doc-tors-note/

[28]"Few Rewards: An agenda to give America's working poor a raise." 2016. Oxfam. https://www.oxfamamerica.org/explore/research-publications/few-rewards/

[29]Adamczyk, Alicia. 2019. "Full-time minimum wage workers cannot afford a 2-bedroom rental anywhere in the US." *CNBC*. https://www.cnbc.com/2019/06/26/minimum-wage-workers-cannot-afford-2-bedroom-rental-anywhere-in-the-us.html

[30]"Number of specialty coffee shops in the United States from 1991 to 2015." 2016. Statista. https://www.statista.com/statistics/196590/total-number-of-snack-and-coffee-shops-in-the-us-since-2002/

[31]"US Coffee Shop Market in Numbers." 2019. Allegra World Coffee Portal. https://www.worldcoffeeportal.com/MediaLibrary/WorldCoffeePortal/WCP-Downloads/Infographics/WCP-USA-2020-infogs.pdf?ext=.pdf

[32]"Coffee." 2020. Statista. https://www.statista.com/outlook/30010000/109/coffee/united-states

[33]Sedacca, Matthew. 2019. "Why Baristas All Over the Country Are Telling Each Other Their Salaries." Eater. https://www.eater.com/young-guns-rising-stars/2019/10/29/20929547/baristas-pay-transparency-crowdsourcing-movement *Note*: to calculate the annual salary listed, the average hourly salary for a barista of $11.17 was multiplied by 2,080 hours. The housing expense amount shown is calculated at 30 percent of the average monthly wage.

[34]Brown, Nick. 2013. "Hawaii Coffee Companies Charged with Widespread Labor Violations." Daily Coffee News. https://dailycoffeenews.com/2013/02/22/hawaii-coffee-companies-charged-with-widespread-labor-violations/

[35]"Number of smartphones sold to end users worldwide from 2007 to 2020." 2019. Statista. https://www.statista.com/statistics/263437/global-smartphone-sales-to-end-users-since-2007/

[36]Apple Engineer Salaries. 2020. Glassdoor. https://www.glassdoor.com/Monthly-Pay/Apple-Engineer-Monthly-Pay-E1138_D_KO6,14.htm

[37]Huang, Echo. 2019. "In China's 'iPhone City,' overtime is used for both punishment and reward.' *Quartz*. https://qz.com/work/1705146/china-labor-watch-foxconns-apple-iphone-factory-breaks-laws-on-temp-workers-overtime/

[38]"Athleisure Market Size, Share & Trends Analysis Report By Product (Mass, Premium), By Distribution Channel (Offline, Online), By Region (North America, Europe, APAC, CSA, MEA), And Segment Forecasts, 2019-2025." 2019. Grand View Research. https://www.grandviewresearch.com/industry-analysis/athleisure-market

[39]Huoh, Ruth. 2017. *Fashion Design: Clothing as Art*.

[40]Semega, J., Kollar, M., Creamer, J., and Mohanty, A. 2019. "Income and Poverty in the United States: 2018." United States Census Bureau. https://census.gov/library/publications/2019/demo/p60-266.html

[41]Denavas-Walt, C. and Proctor. B.D. 2015. "Income and Poverty in the United States: 2014." United States Census Bureau. https://www.census.gov/library/publications/2015/demo/p60-252.html

[42]"Poverty." 2019. The World Bank. https://www.worldbank.org/en/topic/poverty/overview

[43]"FAQs: Global Poverty Line Update." 2015. The World Bank. https://www.worldbank.org/en/topic/poverty/brief/global-poverty-line-faq

[44]"Median Income by Country 2020." 2020. World Population Review. http://worldpopulationreview.com/countries/median-income-by-country/

[45]Erdmann, Kevin. 2019. "Income Tax Benefits to Homeowners Are Regressive." The Bridge, Mercatus Center. https://www.mercatus.org/bridge/commentary/income-tax-benefits-homeowners-are-regressive

[46]"7 Startling Facts: An Up Close Look at Church Attendance in America." 2018. *Outreach*. https://churchleaders.com/pastors/pastor-articles/139575-7-startling-facts-an-up-close-look-at-church-attendance-in-america.html

[47]"The Ultimate List of Charitable Giving Statistics for 2018." 2018. Nonprofit Source. https://nonprofitssource.com/online-giving-statistics/

[48]Holmes, Mike. 2016. "What Would Happen if the Church Tithed?" *Relevant*. https://relevantmagazine.com/love-and-money/what-would-happen-if-church-tithed#wOsGRtY2QEp96d4i.99

[49]"Policy Basics: The Supplemental Nutrition Assistance Program (SNAP)." 2019. Center on Budget and Policy Priorities. https://www.cbpp.org/research/food-assistance/policy-basics-the-supplemental-nutrition-assistance-program-snap

[50]"Fiscal Year 2021 Budget in Brief." 2020. U.S. Department of Housing and Urban Development. https://www.hud.gov/sites/dfiles/CFO/documents/Budgetin-Brief_2020-02_06_Online.pdf

[51]"The Temporary Assistance for Needy Families (TANF) Block Grant: Responses to Frequently Asked Questions." 2019. Congressional Research Service. https://fas.org/sgp/crs/misc/RL32760.pdf

[52]King, Jr., Martin Luther. 1965. "The Octopus of Poverty"

[53]Source unknown, but attributed to Edward Everett Hale.

Chapter 9

[1]"Culture." Merriam-Webster. https://www.merriam-webster.com/dictionary/culture

[2]Useem, J., & Useem. R. 1963. *Human Organizations*, 22(3).

[3]"Global Summary: An overview of the people groups of the world." 2020. Joshua Project. https://joshuaproject.net/

[4]"Census Bureau Reports at Least 350 Languages Spoken in U.S. Homes." 2015. United States Census Bureau. https://www.census.gov/newsroom/press-releases/2015/cb15-185.html

[5]Lloyd, Stephen. "Christianity and the World of Cultures." Center for Global Christianity & Mission, Boston University School of Theology. http://www.bu.edu/cgcm/annual-theme/christianity-and-the-world-of-cultures/

[6]Weisenfeld, Judith. 2015. "Religion in African American History." *Oxford Research Encyclopedia, American History*. doi:10.1093/acrefore/9780199329175.013.24

[7]Singer, Olivia. 2013. "Liberation Theology in Latin America." Modern Latin America, web supplement for 8th Edition, Brown University Library Center for Digital Scholarship. https://library.brown.edu/create/modernlatinamerica/chapters/chapter-15-culture-and-society/essays-on-culture-and-society/liberation-theology-in-latin-america/

[8]Piacenza, J., & Jones, R.P. 2017. "More Christians See America's Days as 'Christian Nation' Behind Us." PRRI. https://www.prri.org/spotlight/america-christian-nation-trump-inauguration/

[9]"PRRI/The Atlantic Survey, Sept 2016." PRRI. https://www.prri.org/search-survey-questions/

[10]"In U.S., Decline of Christianity Continues at Rapid Pace." 2019. Pew Research Center. https://www.pewforum.org/2019/10/17/in-u-s-decline-of-christianity-continues-at-rapid-pace/

[11]Rabey, Steve. 2019. "Rick Christian leaves literary agency that transformed Christian publishing." *Religion News Service*. https://religionnews.com/2019/03/14/rick-christian-leaves-literary-agency-that-transformed-christian-publishing/

[12]"Heaven is for Real (2014)." The Numbers. https://www.the-numbers.com/movie/Heaven-is-for-Real#tab=summary

[13]McCracken, Brett. 2017. *Uncomfortable: The Awkward and Essential Challenge of Christian Community*.

[14]Miller, Dave. 2006. "America, Christianity, and the Culture War (Part I)." Apologetics Press. https://apologeticspress.org/apcontent.aspx?category=7&article=1847

[15]Eberstadt, Mary. 2016. *It's Dangerous to Believe: Religious Freedom and Its Enemies*.

[16]Starnes, Todd. 2014. *God Less America: Real Stories From the Front Lines of the Attack on Traditional Values.*

[17]Nieuwhof, Carey. 2016. "5 Ways Christians Can Approach the Rapidly Changing Moral Culture." https://careynieuwhof.com/5-ways-christians-can-approach-the-rapidly-changing-moral-culture/

[18]Lyons, Gabe. 2008. "Cultural Influence: An Opportunity for the Church. *Comment.* https://www.cardus.ca/comment/article/cultural-influence-an-opportunity-for-the-church/

[19]Wilson, Jared C. 2017. *The Imperfect Disciple: Grace for People Who Can't Get Their Act Together.*

[20]Bellan, Rebecca. 2019. "$23 Billion Education Funding Report Reveals Less Money for City Kids." *CityLab.* https://www.citylab.com/equity/2019/03/education-nonwhite-urban-school-districts-funding-tax/585691/

[21]"Pedestrian Counts." 2020. Times Square NYC. https://www.timessquarenyc.org/do-business/market-research-data/pedestrian-counts

[22]"International tourism, number of departures." The World Bank. https://data.worldbank.org/indicator/ST.INT.DPRT

[23]"Pearl: San Antonio, Texas." American Planning Association. https://www.planning.org/greatplaces/neighborhoods/2017/pearl/

[24]"Press & News." Hotel Emma. https://www.thehotelemma.com/press/

[25]"History and People." Christ Church. https://www.christchurchphila.org/history/

[26]"The Tallest Building in New York City." 2017. Trinity Church Wall Street. https://www.trinitywallstreet.org/blogs/archives/tallest-building-new-york-city

[27]Renn, Aaron. 2014. "Erasing Distinctions." *Sacred Architecture Journal*, 25.

[28]White, Jr., Dan. 2019. Twitter. https://twitter.com/danwhitejr/status/1141718398726004736?s=21

Chapter 10

[1]Carter, Matt. 2017. "Committed to Covenant Community." The Austin Stone Community Church, Austin, Texas (Sermon). https://austinstone.org/resources/sermons/?sapurl=LytlZGM3L21lZGlhL21pLyt1OWJjcWNyP2JyYW5kaW5nPXRydWUmZW1iZWQ9dHJ1ZQ==

[2]Bruno, Dave. 2010. *The 100 Thing Challenge: How I Got Rid of Almost Everything, Remade My Life, and Regained My Soul.*

CPSIA information can be obtained
at www.ICGtesting.com
Printed in the USA
LVHW020017300620
659354LV00004B/1051

9 780578 630083